MASTERING GOLF'S
TOUGHEST SHOTS

MASTERING GOLF'S TOUGHEST SHOTS

The World's Best Caddies Share Their Secrets of Success

By JAMES Y. BARTLETT &
the PROFESSIONAL CADDIES ASSOCIATION

Foreword by **Gary Player** • Preface by **Alfred "Rabbit" Dyer**

SELLERS
PUBLISHING

Published by Sellers Publishing, Inc.

Copyright © 2012 The Caddie Association (TCA) LLC
All rights reserved.

Sellers Publishing, Inc.
161 John Roberts Road, South Portland, Maine 04106
Visit our Web site: www.sellerspublishing.com • E-mail: rsp@rsvp.com

ISBN: 13: 978-1-4162-0690-3
e-ISBN: 978-1-4162-0714-6
Library of Congress Control Number: 2011935641

10 9 8 7 6 5 4 3 2 1

Printed and bound in China.

Photo credits: All photographs by Steve Dinberg / PCA Foundation Library, with the following
exceptions: Cover: Black Knight International Archives, used by permission; pps. 6, 7, 154, 157:
PCA Media Hall of Fame Library; p. 15: Doug Kapustin/MCT via Getty Images; pps. 16, 35: George
Hewitson Photography / PCA Media Library; pps. 31, 55, 149: Black Knight International Archives; p.
41: Brian Losness — US PRESSWIRE; p. 51: Mike Nelson Photography / PCA Media HOF Library;
p. 80: Dennis Cone, Stu Walls, Joe Lambert / PCA Media Library; p. 90: John Stewart; p. 103: Michael
Sackett — US PRESSWIRE; pps. 129, 152: Rachel Owen — www.imageicon.com / PCA Media HOF
Library; p. 133: Bob DeChiara — US PRESSWIRE; p. 151: Kevin Allen / PCA Media HOF Library.

CONTENTS

PREFACE

BY Alfred "Rabbit" Dyer

Alfred "Rabbit" Dyer, PCA Caddie Hall of Fame caddie

I have been blessed to be a caddie! I started at the age of nine as a ball boy at Metalrie Country Club in New Orleans in 1946. Ten years later, I was a caddie working for Gary Player on the PGA Tour and I thank him. Life was different back then. Caddies took Greyhound buses to tournaments, slept four to a room or at the "Underwood Hotel" in the local town. We were a band of guys who showed up, shut up, and stayed up each week in order to get the greatest seat in the house being inside the ropes. I have traveled the world, put my son through Princeton University, have met and caddied for presidents and other dignitaries, celebrities, heads of corporations, multi- millionaires, and people of all ages and backgrounds. I have even had the opportunity to play some of the great courses I worked. But the greatest accomplishment I have had over the years is to see caddies receiving recognition in the game of golf. In 2000, I was inducted into the Professional Caddies Association Caddie Hall of Fame, along with other good caddies, and I'm currently a PCA Hall of Fame ambassador to the PCA Worldwide. I thank Laura and Dennis Cone for what they do to help ALL caddies.

Older golfers will know the long history of the caddie and their contribution to the game over the years. After all, the first professional golfers were caddies. I did not play golf to caddie; I caddied and learned how to play golf. I also quickly learned that caddying could be my chance to change my life. Who knew back then where it would take me or that I would make it my career that would last over 50 years? Once I had my chance to carry that bag, there was no turning back.

Golf is a game that was meant to be played to have fun, promote competition, and be enjoyed by anyone willing to take the time to understand and walk the course. Take a friend, carry your own or a friend's bag, or even better yet, hire a caddie and learn how to train your "inner caddie." Let's all get behind the PCA Caddie Comeback and help the kids get on the golf course, so they can learn life, and social and business skills, while growing the game we love for future generations.

Alfred "Rabbit" Dyer
PCA Caddie Ambassador and 2000 Caddie Hall of Fame inductee

FOREWORD

BY Gary Player

I have been so fortunate to work with many great caddies throughout my over 50 years as a professional golfer. Sometimes on my far-flung travels, I would simply take the best available local caddie at the club where we were playing: and on other occasions I might have a friend in that city who enjoyed being "on my bag" for the week.

Gary Player and Alfred "Rabbit" Dyer team up for another win!

Having said this, I really had only two men who caddied regularly for me: Alfred "Rabbit" Dyer on the PGA Tour and Bobby Verwey, Jr. on the Champions Tour. Both of them took the time to learn my game and what we needed to do to win, which are essential to being a good caddie. They are special men, who traveled the world with me, and I consider them both friends and a meaningful part of my success.

The image of a caddie that you see on TV is of someone lugging a huge bag around the course, tending the pin, and helping to read putts, but that is not the real role that a caddie plays. Caddies are an important part of a professional's success because if you have a good caddie, he or she can help you develop and execute a strategic plan that helps you win. They are part friend, part adviser. They are part cheerleader and part psychologist.

When we arrived at a tournament, Rabbit and Bobby would walk the course during the practice rounds and really pay attention to the setup and, most important, how the greens were playing. We would discuss each hole and develop a strategy that made sense for my game. It was important for me to tailor an approach to take advantage of my strengths and, after 165 global victories and 18 Major Championships (nine on the Regular Tour and nine on the Senior Tour), I'd say we did a pretty good job. Most certainly, I know one thing for sure: I could not have done it without them.

I am pleased to be able to contribute to *Mastering Golf's Toughest Shots* and to help the Professional Caddies Association (PCA) recognize the contributions caddies have made to this wonderful game of golf, which has brought us all such great joy, rewards, and happiness. I hope the game does the same for you.

Best wishes,
GARY PLAYER

The Trouble with Golf Is Trouble

If you could kick the person in the pants responsible for most of your trouble, you wouldn't sit for a month.
— *Theodore Roosevelt*

Trouble is a major part of the game of golf. We'd like to imagine that our game consists of an unbroken string of good swings, balls that hug the centerline of the tightly mown fairways, putts for a birdie on every hole, and nothing but blue skies and candy all the way around. Unfortunately, it doesn't work out that way. Ever.

The world's best players and their caddies know that scoring in golf is all about controlling the extent of one's mistakes. They know that stuff happens in almost every round. A rogue gust of wind might push a ball sideways or knock it out of the sky. A car may backfire at the top of one's backswing. A well-struck ball may hit an unseen rock or sprinkler head and careen away in an unintended direction. At the same time, the physical moves required to deliver the clubface squarely into the back of the ball at a swing speed of 100 mph or faster are complicated, and the slightest, most microscopic variation can send the ball on an entirely unintended flight pattern — into the trees, the rough, the bunker, or the desert.

So the combination of what the rulemakers call "the rub of the green" (i.e., "luck") and our own swing imperfections (and everyone up to and including Tiger Woods has them) inevitably will result in a golfer facing a so-called "trouble" shot during his round; that is, a ball that ends up in a place where you didn't intend for it to go. Those of us who are high handicappers will face a tough shot to get out of trouble perhaps once a hole. Others, like the pros, only find themselves off the comfortable and beaten path a few times per round. But it happens to everyone.

But the question — and the point, really, of this book — is *what do you do when you find yourself in trouble on the golf course? Or facing a tough shot? Or a shot that requires something other than a normal swing? Or when the pressure is on, the stakes are high, and money is on the line?*

Opposite page: Whenever Phil Mickelson finds himself in trouble, his caddie Jim "Bones" Mackay is there to help him find a way out.

Most of the time, we choke. Faced with trouble and pressure, brainlock sets in and our blood pressure, breathing rate, and decision making speeds up. In the heat of the moment, we often choose to play a shot that represents the worst possible option. More often than not, we end up making matters worse and, at the end of the hole, we're forced to write down on the scorecard a double- or triple-bogey, a snowman, or the dreaded "X."

Why do we do this to ourselves? Well, it's only human to try to overcome adversity, or make up for a mistake or a stroke of bad luck, with a miraculous recovery. Even if we know, in the back of our minds, that the percentages are against us and our chances of success are slim, we're likely to cast caution to the wind and go for broke.

We do this, in short, *because we don't think like a caddie.* Imagine playing with a caddie who meets you at the fairway bunker where your ball sits in a dicey lie close to the elevated front lip. Your caddie glances at the situation and says, "You've got about 190 yards to the green. Here, take this 3-iron and give it a whack. You're gonna have to hit it pretty clean to get it up and over the lip. So I'd grip it hard and swing as fast as you can."

Or maybe he meets you deep in the woods, where your ball lies on some pine straw with nothing but tree trunks and branches between you and the green. "Hmmm," he says this time. "Well, they say trees are 90 percent air. Take the sand wedge and whack it. I'll bet you get through."

Or you've got a long putt on the 18th green and you need to get it down in two to win the match. Your caddie hands you the putter and says, "You know, it would be much more dramatic if you sank this one. The heck with lagging it close . . . I'd aim straight for the hole and hit it hard to take the break out."

That kind of advice, of course, is **not** what caddies usually offer. Caddies usually don't waste too much time bemoaning the fates or the bad swings that got their player into trouble; nor do they worry about making up for lost ground with one swing. Caddies think about only the shot at hand, the immediate problem that must be solved. They don't care how you got there, or whether you're in the middle of the fairway or deep in the rough. The only problem at hand is how to advance the ball toward the hole with the purpose of making the lowest possible score.

Sometimes, that means a caddie will advise his player **not** to advance the ball at the hole. That's because the elements at that moment — the lie, the weather conditions, the terrain, or the challenge of the shot — argue against everything else except getting the ball safely back into play. In the interest of making the lowest possible score, which after all is the point of the game, experienced caddies know that sometimes the conservative play, the layup, the get-it-on-the-fairway-again sideways chip, is often the best alternative.

Professional golfers, of course, *hate* to lay it up. They don't want to be accused of cowardice, as Chip Beck was in the 1993 Masters when, in the heat of the battle for the tournament on Sunday afternoon, he elected not to challenge the pond in front of the 15th green with his second shot, instead meekly laying it up. (He made par and lost the tournament.) Look at Phil Mickelson, who goes for everything (even when he probably shouldn't). Like that miracle shot at the 2010 Masters on the par-5 13th, when he went for the green from a sidehill lie on the pine straw, surrounded by trees and their hanging boughs. He made it onto the green, and the TV announcers immediately termed it a "one-in-a-million" shot. While it's no doubt true that you could line up a million high-handicapped hackers and perhaps one or two of them would be able to hit a golf ball onto that well-guarded green from the same position, for players like Mickelson, who do nothing else but practice and play golf, the chances for success are a bit higher. Professionals go for it more often because they possess experience, knowledge, the ability to control their golf ball, and the confidence that they can purposefully make the right swing at the right time. Most of the rest of us do not.

Did Jim "Bones" Mackay, Phil's caddie, recommend that Mickelson try that shot at that moment on Sunday afternoon at the Masters? I'm sure he at least had one or two alternatives to suggest, including chipping the ball out safely and trying to make a birdie with his wedge and his putter. But I'm also sure that once Mickelson pulled his 6-iron and said, "I'm going for it," Bones quickly agreed with his man, reassured him he could do it, and told him to keep his head down, or whatever last words of encouragement he typically utters. The caddie's main job, after all, is to make sure his player hits every shot with the utmost confidence.

Unfortunately, most of us don't play regularly with caddies, and our motorized golf carts don't offer much in the way of advice. But *every* golfer should take the time to think like a caddie before making a shot, especially when the ball is in trouble and the heat is on. In our last book, *Think Like a Caddie, Play Like a Pro,* we talked about how to think like a caddie: gathering the important data required to make every shot successful.

That kind of detached, calm, and reasoned analysis is even more important when the shot at hand is either out of the ordinary or made under conditions of tension and stress. Caddies think about only one shot at a time: the one that must next be played. How the ball got to its current position is totally unimportant. How to get the ball to the next target is all that's important. Nothing else matters.

Thus, when presented with the fairway bunker situation cited above, the player may be thinking about trying a hybrid 3-iron. But the caddie is likely pulling a wedge or sand wedge and looking for a suitable target in the fairway in front of the green, from whence a nice, easy shot will get the ball onto the green with a chance for par and a bogey at worst. From the deep woods a caddie will be scouting the best, tree-free route to get the ball back into the open, back into play. And on those last green pressure putts, the caddie will be considering only the proper line and the right speed to get the ball near the hole. If it happens to fall in, great. But to win the match, the ball must finish close to the hole. That's the target for that shot.

The emphasis of this book, then, is how to *think* your way around a golf course, selecting appropriate targets for your golfing ability, and choosing to make shots you *know* you can make, not shots you *hope* will come off successfully. The difference between the two is the difference from playing to your handicap or better, or shooting scores in the 90s and 100s.

As in our last book, we have called on the collective wisdom of some of the game's best caddies, including both those who are still looping on the professional tours, and those ensconced in the World Caddie Hall of Fame of the Professional Caddies Association. None of the advice these experts have offered will tell you *how* to hit the tough shots; as one veteran of more than 40 years on the tours said, "Hey, it's not my job to hit the shot. My guy gets paid millions to do that."

Instead, these expert caddies offer their players facts about the shot to be played: the yardage, the conditions, the wind, the alternatives. And that's the kind of strategic thinking that helps a player to make the right shot decisions, to avoid getting deeper in trouble, and to make the best score.

In the following pages, you'll learn how to think like a caddie to make the tough shots — how to survey the shot at hand, consider the various alternatives, and choose the right club and the right shot to get out of trouble and get back in the game.

CHAPTER ONE

Give Yourself a Hand:
Five Fingers to Analyze Every Tough Shot

During the 2011 U.S. Open at Congressional Country Club in Bethesda, Maryland, Northern Ireland's Rory McIlroy was asked by the media how he could explain his record-setting performance that led to his winning the tournament with an unprecedented 16 under-par score.

"All I'm trying to do," he said, midway through the tournament when he was leading by ten strokes, "is make aggressive shots toward my target."

If there was ever a one-sentence definition of how to play winning golf, that rather simple summation is it. *Make aggressive shots toward your target.*

Now Rory McIlroy is one of the handful of best players on the planet. But his strategy is one that can and should be adopted by every golfer, no matter what one's handicap, experience level, or what kind of shot one is facing. Make an aggressive shot toward your target.

That also happens to be an excellent description of what most professional caddies encourage their players to do. Ask any caddie what his main job description is, and you'll get some variation of answer along the lines of "Make sure my player is confident about the shot he's about to hit." You cannot make an aggressive swing toward your target if you're not confident about the planned result of that shot. And you can only be truly confident if you know you're about to play a shot that's within your ability

Rory McIlroy makes an aggressive swing to his target at the U.S. Open at Congressional Country Club in 2011.

Opposite page: Jack Nicklaus is considered one of the best ever at course management and strategic thinking.

level and will get the ball where you want it to go — to your target.

Rory McIlroy hits practice shots by the hour and has played thousands of competitive rounds of golf, many under the white-hot glare of tournament pressure. So, his level of confidence when standing over a shot may be worlds apart from those of us who play a game that can charitably be called "hit and hope." But the Rules of Golf do not demand that the rest of us must attempt to copy Rory McIlroy's superior game of golf. Indeed, to even attempt to hit a shot like Rory, considering his young age (he was born in 1989), physical condition, customized equipment, years of experience, and God-given talent, would be the height of folly. We can certainly try to mimic his golf swing, as beautiful as it is, but not his choice and execution of shots.

Even more, we should all take to heart his basic course strategy: Make an aggressive shot at your target. Because that will mean we've selected targets that our level of talent can deliver.

LPGA pro Andrea Knox makes an aggressive shot at Florida's beautiful Black Diamond Ranch.

That we've planned our way around our own golf course, based on our abilities, and that every shot we attempt is a shot we know we can make. Consider how much confidence you have when standing over a 200-yard shot with a 3-iron or hybrid club. Usually not that much. The list of things that can go wrong fill the mind with worry and doubt, and the results are usually less than optimal. Now envision a 100-yard shot with a pitching wedge. No problem, right? Even if your pitching wedge has to fly over some bunkers or a pond or some other kind of trouble, most of the time you know you can easily make that shot, and your swing is usually free and easy and stress free, i.e., *confident*. How much better could you score if you could stand over *every* shot with the same kind of confidence you have for that 100-yard pitch?

In our first book, *Think Like a Caddie, Play Like a Pro,* we described how a golfer can shoot better scores by doing the same things a professional caddie would do: map out a golf course, develop a plan of attack, and then execute that plan one shot at a time by considering the pertinent data (lie, wind, yardage, and conditions) and selecting the correct club to get the ball from its current position to its intended target. This book will concentrate on the tough and troublesome shots one can encounter in a round of golf, using that same basic strategic approach. The way out of trouble is the same as the ordinary shot from the fairway: select an appropriate target (the best one available given the situation you're in), plan to make the best shot you can, and make a confident swing. Indeed, when you find your ball in a difficult or unusual place — in the bunker, under the trees, buried in deep rough — it's imperative to step back, analyze the situation, determine the alternatives, and select the shot that will best get you out of trouble and back into play.

When caddies follow their player into trouble, the *last* thing they think about is the yardage to the target. Instead, they look at the lie and ask, "Can we get a club on the ball? How much loft do we need to get out of here?" They look at the path of the shot and ask, "How will the ball come out of this lie? Hot? With spin or without? What will happen when the ball lands?" They consider the wind, other hazards that may be in the way, and the shape and trajectory the shot must take. Once all of those questions have been answered, the caddie is ready to recommend a target for the shot and a club to get the ball to that target. In the professional game, of course, the player almost always wants to go for it. But they have the game and the experience to pull off even the most difficult trouble shot. In the world of the amateur hacker, "going for it" is usually a heroic and foolhardy choice. And we don't usually have a caddie on the bag to recommend a safer, more makeable recovery shot.

Whether you are making a shot from the tee box, from the fairway, from the deep rough, or on the putting green, you must first collect the data you need, to know what kind of shot you need to play. If you played with a caddie, it would be his job to give you these necessary and important pieces of information. But since most of us do not play with caddies, here is what you need to consider *before* deciding what shot you want to make and which club you will select to do it. It's a memory device to help you remember the information you need and its importance in the shot decision. We call this:

THE CADDIE'S FIVE-FINGER FORMAT

1. Thumb. The thumb is the strongest and most important of your fingers, without which almost nothing else would be possible. And the most important piece of pre-shot data to collect is, first and foremost, **the target**. As you get ready to hit a shot, whether it's the first one of the day or the 99th, you must first decide where you want the ball to go. Now while this sounds overly simplistic — obviously you want your tee shots to go into the fairway, you want your approach shots to go onto the green, and you want your putts to go into the hole — better players and their caddies know that selecting *specific* targets is one of the secrets to shooting lower scores.

From the tee, you want to select your target — not *just* "the fairway," but a specific part of the fairway: left side, right side, short of that fairway bunker, a sunny patch of grass, a shadow, or that place where the mowing pattern changes . . . be as specific as you can be in selecting your target.

Don't slip into the bad habit of choosing a reverse target, that is, the place you really, really *don't* want to go. "OK, don't dub this one — there's nothing but wilderness between me and the fairway." "Whatever you do, don't go right into that big lake!" "Gotta clear that big bunker on the left." When your mind is full of thoughts about all the trouble spots, your brain begins to get a message that you really want your ball to go there, and it helpfully complies by producing a shot that sends the ball there. Instead, mentally picture your ball successfully arriving at your target, which should be the perfect place for your next shot.

Likewise, on approach shots, don't think of your target as being "on the green," or "right at the flag." Instead, pick a specific part of the green: center, left, right, front, or back. Again, select some part of the target that stands out visually and put that visual in the forefront of your mind. (As you get closer to the green, the hole itself can be used as the target.)

Even when you're putting, you should have a target. Putting is all line and speed. The line is the direction in which you start the putt. That requires a target: a ball mark, a discolored piece of grass, the edge of the hole . . . something you can *aim at*. When you get closer to the hole, say from three feet or less, your target should not be "the hole"; that's still too generic. Pick out a *particular blade of grass* on the edge of the cup and try to roll your ball over that blade on its way into the hole.

There's no such thing as getting too specific when selecting your target. And you can't make a confident swing at the ball unless you know *exactly* where you want that ball to go. The first

Caddie Ted Scott points the way to the target for his man, Bubba Watson.

step should always be the most important: choose your target.

2. Pointer. After selecting a specific target, point at the ball with your second finger and consider **the lie**. Obviously, if your ball is sitting on its peg on the tee or resting comfortably in the middle of the fairway, you can quickly check this one off and move on to the next finger. But other times, especially when the ball is off the fairway, you will need to examine the lie and determine if it will allow you to advance the ball to your selected target.

If your ball is sitting down in deep rough and your target is 190 yards away, something's got to give. If your ball ends up with one of those "fried egg" lies in a bunker (that is, when the ball comes to rest in its own impact mark, thus resembling the yolk of a fried egg surrounded by a circle of sand, i.e., the "white"), it's going to be harder to control than a ball sitting nicely on the sand. A severe uphill, downhill, or sidehill lie will also affect the planned shot.

So the pointer finger determines if it is possible, considering how the ball is lying, to get it to the selected target. If yes, move on to the next finger. If no, go back and choose another, more appropriate, target.

3. Middle finger. The longest finger means you find out how far away you are from the target. This is the time to determine **the yardage** to your target and think about which club will move the ball that distance. Notice that this is not the first piece of data to be collected. This will seem contrary to the way most of us play: get to the ball, find out the yardage to the green, and pull a club that typically goes about that distance.

That's not how a caddie thinks. A caddie's first thought is, "Where are we going with this next shot?" (And where do we want to go with the one after that?) Once the target is selected, the caddie will look at the lie to make sure it's possible to get there. Then, and only then, will the caddie calculate the distance to the target. Again, it makes no sense to figure out a yardage until you know *exactly where you want the ball to go.*

For instance, let's say you hit a good drive down the fairway, and as you drive up in your cart, you see the ball is lying next to the 150-yard marker. "Great," you think to yourself as you pull your 7-iron, the club that usually goes about 150 yards.

But a caddie would look up at the green and see where the pin has been cut (every day, the hole is moved to a different position on the green by the greenskeepers — sometimes it's in the front, sometimes in the back, sometimes in the center). If it's toward the back of the green, the caddie will know this shot has to carry an additional ten yards to get back to the pin. That's his target: *back of the green.* Since the lie is good, the caddie will check the pin sheet and see the pin is cut 12 paces back from center. That means a distance of 150 to the center, but 162 yards back to the hole location. That's a different club — say an easy 6-iron.

Get into the habit of choosing the target first, and then select the club that will get the ball to that target's distance.

4. Ring finger. The second-longest finger serves as a memory device to remind you to consider the **conditions.** Most important of these is the wind. A golf ball weighs just 1.62 ounces, and even a gentle breeze will affect the ball's flight one way or another. Most amateur golfers grossly underestimate the influence of the wind. That 162-yard approach shot described above? If the wind is in your face, the playing distance might be 172 yards, which would call for a 5-iron. That's quite a bit different from the 7-iron you pulled without thinking the shot through, and a two-club mistake might mean the difference between putting for a birdie and trying to get up-and-down for a bogey.

Other conditions to consider include:

- **The weather.** Is it cold and damp? Hot and humid? Raining or clear? How will the atmospheric conditions affect the flight of your ball?

- **The terrain.** You might have a flat lie, but is the target down- or uphill? You've got to add in allowances for going uphill, and subtract yardage for going down.

- **Shot shape.** You might have a tree to go around, or want to shape a shot left or right to take advantage of the wind conditions.

- **The target.** How will the ball react once it gets to the target? Is the green hard or receptive? Can you fly it in or does the target require a rolling approach? Is the fairway canted one way or the other? Is it soft or hard? All these things will affect the outcome of your shot and so must be considered.

5. Pinky finger. Finally, use the reminder of the smallest finger to consider **the situation.** While it's true that every shot is important, it's also true that some shots are more important than others, depending on the kind of game or competition you're playing. If it's just you and the guys out for your weekly Nassau, and it's the 1st hole, then you can relax and just play your best shot. If it's the 18th hole and the money is riding on you winning the hole, then you should take some extra care to double-check your decision, and maybe run through the Five-Finger Format one more time.

One should rarely let the situation determine the shot (instead of the target and lie), but in those few times when it's important to the match, it doesn't hurt to remind yourself to concentrate and select the best possible shot to match the circumstance. If you're between clubs, or slightly uncertain, the pinky finger should remind you to take the extra club or make sure your target is precise, so you can make your shot with confidence.

Always remember that there is no "correct" way to play a hole. The score you write down on the card is the same if, for instance, on a par 4 you hit driver, 4-iron, and two putts, or if you hit 3-wood, 8-iron, sand wedge, and one putt. The great golf iconoclast Moe Norman once came to a par-4 hole and asked the distance. "It's a drive and 9-iron," he was told by his caddie. "OK," he said, and hit his tee shot with his 9-iron. Then he hit his approach shot onto the green from the fairway with his driver. "Guess you were right," Moe said.

High-handicap players tend to get lost by trying to play holes "in regulation," that is, one shot to reach the green of a par 3, two shots for a par 4, and three for a par 5. There's no law that says you can't lay up on a par-3 hole, especially if it's a long, difficult hole, and you're not comfortable trying to hit a long iron or a fairway wood (whose accuracy is always tough to control). Instead, identify a target in some safe, open place around the green, hit a comfortable and confident shot there, and then pitch or chip the ball to the green, hoping for a one-putt par or, at worst, a two-putt bogey. You may undergo some ribbing from your playing partners, but playing smart, confident, strategic golf, and consistently making those aggressive shots to your target, means you're much more likely to have the last laugh when the scores are totted up in the 19th-hole lounge.

Montana Thompson, a longtime PGA Tour caddie, recalls the two different strategies he and Billy Mayfair adopted on the 18th hole at the 1998 Nissan Los Angeles Open at the Valencia Country Club.

> ## WHEN SHOULD A PLAYER GAMBLE ON A SHOT?
>
> *When I don't think a player can make a shot, I try to get them to play smart. Here at Seminole, on No. 3, the par 5, we have a lot of members who want to take a 3-wood, but it's very narrow by the green and it takes a perfect shot to get home safely. I will suggest that they take an iron and lay up 100 yards short. We can make a birdie or par, which is better than a 6 or 7 from a bad place. Sometimes I win that argument, and sometimes I lose.*
>
> *– Eli Brown*
> *Longtime caddie at Seminole Country Club, Florida, and PCA Hall of Famer*

HOW WE PULL A CLUB

When the caddie and his player are working well together, there will be a consistent pattern to their discussions of each shot. You don't start talking about playing the shot until you get down near the ball — let [the player] have his downtime walking between shots. You can chat about other things — sports, dinner last night, whatever. As you get near the ball, you start preparing. The caddie gets the yardage and then the player and the caddie evaluate the lie. Then you check the wind and decide on the target. Last step is to agree on the shot — trajectory, shape, spin — and pull the club that he needs. So it's yardage, lie, wind, target, type of shot, and then club.

— Dean Elliott
PGA Tour caddie

"We came to the last hole needing a birdie to tie Tiger Woods for the lead. Billy hit a good drive, but that last hole at Valencia is a long par 5 and the fairway slants hard to the right, so instead of trying to knock it on with a long iron from a hanging lie [when the ball comes to rest on the side of a hill, either above or below the feet], and possibly putting ourselves in a tough up-and-down situation, we decided to lay it up to Billy's comfortable sand wedge distance in front of the green. He laid it up, knocked his sand wedge on, and made the putt — and we're off to the playoff.

"In the playoff, on the same 18th hole, Tiger got in a little trouble off the tee and had to lay up with his second shot. This time, from about the same place in the fairway, we decided to try and hit the ball in the front left bunker on our approach. Now Ken Venturi was up in the TV booth saying that was the absolutely worst place we could be. But we didn't want to miss the green to the right. And we knew that Billy had a great sand game. Sure enough, he hit it tight, made the birdie putt, and won the tournament, the only time Tiger ever lost a playoff on the PGA Tour."

In other words, Mayfair twice put his ball in a position from which he could make an aggressive shot to his target: the first time, to a comfortable wedge distance; the second time, into a bunker. And, because he's a professional with a great short game, he could then make aggressive and comfortable shots from those two positions to the green.

It doesn't always work out quite that way. Jack Nicklaus recalls one year when he had Alvin "DiDi" Gonzalez on the bag at the Crosby Pro-Am at Pebble Beach. On the par-5 2nd hole, Jack hit his tee shot way to the left, almost out of bounds and behind a stand of trees. DiDi recommended Jack take a 5-iron and hit the ball back onto the fairway, thinking there would still be a good chance for a birdie that way. But Jack wanted to curve a 3-wood around the trees and go for the green. They argued. Jack won. "I hit the 3-wood, hooked it around the trees, and it finished a foot or two from the hole," Jack recalls. "I turned to DiDi and said, 'How was that?' He looked at me and said, 'The 5-iron was the right play!'"

At the 1986 British Open at Turnberry, Greg Norman was leading on the final day. And then on the 7th hole, he duck-hooked his drive deep into the rough. His caddie, Pete Bender, knew something was wrong. "I've almost never seen him hit a shot like that," Bender recalls. "I knew something was wrong, and I tried to think of what to say to him. I finally told him he was playing too fast and needed to slow everything down. He nodded, but then started walking off toward the rough at a fast pace again. I reached out and grabbed his sweater and pulled him back and said, 'Slow down! You're the best player here and you're going to win this thing, but you have to slow down and walk at my pace.' Then I told him a joke and got him to laugh, and he finally looked at me and said, 'You're right . . . let's just have some fun!' When he birdied the next hole, I knew he was back."

Most of us don't have a caddie to grab us by the back of the sweater and tell us to slow it down, take our time, stop and smell the roses, or do whatever else it takes to get us to stop worrying and to just play the game one shot at a time. But we can train ourselves to *think* like a caddie, especially when we get ourselves in trouble. We can take an extra moment to take a deep breath, consider the options, and then select the best shot.

Tough Lie, Tournament on the Line . . . What Would *You* Do?

David Toms at the 2001 PGA Championship

David Toms had a problem. It was the final hole of the 2001 PGA Championship at the Atlanta Athletic Club, he was nursing a one-stroke lead over his playing partner, Phil Mickelson, and he was faced with a very tough shot, and an even tougher decision.

His drive on the par-4 closing hole had drifted off to the right and found the first cut of rough. He had 210 yards to the flagstick. A pond lurked in front of the green, and there were bunkers and deep rough behind it. And, just to add a little more drama to the moment, he had a "hanging lie": the ball was on a slight rise, about four inches above his feet.

So Toms and his caddie, Scott Gneiser, talked over the options for the shot.

"It wasn't that bad of a lie in the first cut," Gneiser recalled some years later. "But it was hanging up there above his feet. We both knew his 3-iron wouldn't get there, and he at first pulled his 5-wood. 'What's it like over the green?' he asked. 'Not good,' I told him. Getting up and down for a par from the rough back there would have been tough. And we both could see the water in front. That was lurking in our heads. So I asked him, 'You wanna lay up?' He said, 'Yes.'"

Professional golfers almost never lay up. Not only does that run counter to their DNA, but the pros have a deeper arsenal of shots they can call on, thanks to countless hours of practice and years of tournament experience that has taught them how they react under pressure. Toms and Gneiser knew they needed a par 4 to win the PGA, or at least ensure a playoff in the event that Phil Mickelson, whose ball was safely in the fairway, made a birdie.

"It's like we read each other's mind," Gneiser said. "We both knew the shot wasn't there, with the water in front and the trouble over the green. Going for it could have thrown the tournament away."

So instead, Toms asked Gneiser to give him a club to get the ball to 85 yards from the green, his green-light range for a smooth, 60-degree wedge shot. "His wedge was from 88 yards and he stuck it to about 12 feet," Gneiser said. "We both looked at the putt, we both saw it was outside right, and David just poured it into the cup."

To Gneiser, the decision to lay up was "just taking care of business. If we lay up and he misses the putt, then we're probably in a playoff, not losing the tournament. But David has always been a great wedge player, so we were just playing to our strength."

David Toms (right) with his caddie. Scott Gneiser. at the 2011 PGA Championship.

CHAPTER TWO

Getting to Green: How to Make Every Shot Easy

At some point before every golf shot, you make the go/no-go decision. It comes at that instant when you mentally envision the shot you're about to play and select the club that you think will get the ball where you want it to go. Your brain has taken whatever information about the upcoming shot you have observed, gathered, or considered, processed that information, and spit out an answer: *To successfully make this shot, you need a high 7-iron with a slight draw into the middle the green, and let it roll back to the flag.* When you reach into your golf bag and pull out that 7-iron, you have, whether you know it or not, made a go/no-go decision.

The problem with most of us is that we make that decision both too soon and almost subconsciously, without thinking about what we're doing. Ideally, the go/no-go decision should be made last, before a club is selected, and only after consciously gathering and considering all the pertinent data, which would be provided by your caddie, if you had one.

In that scenario, you'd come up to your ball, and your caddie would be standing there with his course guide open. "What do we have?" you'd say.

"See that shadow in the middle of the green?" he'd say. "That's your target. The pin is another three paces past center, but we've got 152 yards to that shadow, which is perfect. Not much wind, and it's coming out of the right, which is good. Ball's a little above your feet, which is also good. Nice high little draw in there is perfect."

"Sounds like the 7," you'd say.

"I like that club," he'd agree. "Just a good solid swing. Nice and easy."

Your caddie gives you the data: target, lie, wind, and yardage; and you pull the right club. You "picture" the shot mentally

Opposite page: The late Payne Stewart and longtime caddie Mike Hicks at the 1999 U.S. Open.

(see sidebar, Play *Sense*-sational Golf, p. 36) and make that go decision. The proper sequencing of information allows the golfer to make an informed, intelligent choice about how to play the shot. That, in turn, allows one to make the kind of aggressive swing at the target that brings the best results.

Those of us who don't play with caddies often make the go decision too soon, or before gathering enough information. Don't pull a club or decide on the shot until you've gone completely through the Five-Finger Format. Turn the go/no-go moment into a conscious decision, once you've identified the target, considered the lie, calculated the distance and conditions, and thought a moment about the situation. Then you'll know that you've done the preparation necessary to make a successful shot, and you can pull the club with confidence, saying to yourself . . . "Let's GO!"

(Note: Slow play is the bane of golf for everyone. But none of the steps outlined in this book, including the Five-Finger Format, should take more than 10 or 15 seconds to accomplish in the normal course of play. If you're standing around running complicated equations in your head, waiting for divine inspiration, throwing handfuls of grass in the air or otherwise dawdling, you're just going to make your playing partners — and everyone else on the golf course behind you — irritated. Most of the pre-shot planning discussed in this book can be done before you get to your ball or while waiting for your turn to play.)

GREEN-LIGHT SPECIALS

Every now and then, you'll hear one of the TV commentators talking about a shot about to be played by one of the Tour players. "He's got a green-light special here," the announcer will say. By this he means that the player is faced with a shot well within his capabilities, that doesn't have much in the way of trouble to avoid or overcome, and, because the club selected is one the player is especially adept at, the expectation is that the player ought to be able to get the shot pretty close to the hole.

A lot of shots we face during a round can be termed "green light." These are all the fairly straightforward shots from the fairway and tee, plus almost all the short-game pitches, chips, and putts. All these green-light shots are generally pretty simple shots with nothing much to worry about between you and the target.

But frequently, especially with high handicappers, we are faced with a yellow-light shot. Perhaps you're a distance from the target that means you'll need to select a particular iron, hybrid, or fairway club you're not comfortable using or have had trouble with before. That internal unease flips the switch to yellow. Or maybe you're slightly behind a tree and the only really good shot selection calls for you to draw the ball around the right side of the tree. But you don't or can't hit a draw. That's a yellow light. Any time you are faced with a situation that's a little different, a little uncommon, or a little tricky, those are the times to think yellow. And that means think again, make sure you are confident about the shot, and make sure you can make that aggressive swing to your target. If you can't do that, then select another target and go there.

Every shot you make during a round should be a green-light shot.

This sounds ridiculously simple. But think back over your last round or two, and you should be able to easily recall more than a few shots you made

Gary Player always has a green-light shot from a bunker.

that were yellow-light situations. Maybe you weren't sure you had enough club to carry that bunker in front (*did you?*). Maybe you stood over that 3-wood fairway shot and just didn't feel comfortable (*what happened?*).

Maybe you had a little chip shot over a deep bunker to a tight pin and decided to try a Phil Mickelson flop shot that you really haven't practiced that much (*Did you have to play the next one from the sand, or did you blade it over the green?*).

What would have happened to your score if you had decided to take an extra club, lay up with a 5-iron instead of hitting the 3-wood, or just play your usual sand wedge shot? In the last two situations, anyway, you might have been putting for a par instead of a birdie, but you likely wouldn't be making anything worse than a bogey. What scores did you make instead? Double-bogey? Triple? Worse?

Risk/reward is one thing. Playing within your capabilities is quite another, and that's what the color system will help you do. But it will only work — for you — if you resolve to transform every shot and situation to a green light. Select a target, a club, and a shot that you *know* you can make. Eliminate all doubt. Play the course, not the expectations of yourself or anyone else. When you play the game with green-light confidence and assuredness, you will play better golf. When you go ahead with shots that raise feelings of doubt, anxiety, or fear, bad things are almost certain to occur.

Lee Trevino once was forced to play an entire round at the British Open relying only on his caddie's green-light sense. He had never used Willie Aitchison before, and Trevino only discovered his situation when they arrived at his ball in the first fairway. "What've we got?" Lee asked Willie. "A 7-iron," Willie answered confidently. "No," Trevino said, "how many yards do we have left?" "I don't do yards," Willie answered. "I just know it's a 7-iron

Lee Trevino (above) won six majors in his career, including one British Open where his caddie, Willie Aitchison, told Lee he "didn't do" yardages.

to the middle of the green." Trevino must have been surprised, but he played that first round without getting a yardage, just discussing and agreeing on the proper club for each shot. At the end of their good round, Trevino congratulated Willie but told him he'd need to get actual yardages from then on. Willie retorted that Lee would have to teach him how then. They went on to win two British Open titles together, at Royal Birkdale in 1971 and at Muirfield in 1972.

And, from time to time, we come across those red-light conditions. The ball's behind a tree, or buried in a bunker, or sitting down in five inches of thick rough. If you can hear the voice of Bob Rosburg saying, "Johnnie . . . he's got no shot, no shot at all," then you should be thinking red. It's not yellow, because there's no way you can extricate yourself from the situation. When you're in the red zone, just take your medicine and look for the best target to get your ball back in play. In other words, look for a green-light shot that will get you out of trouble and back in the game.

Color coding is just another way of determining the risk and reward potential of each shot you make. Golf is a game all about managing and balancing risk vs. reward, and all of us have different thresholds. If you're the chairman of the board of a community bank, you probably tend to be a bit more conservative in taking chances than, say, a high-tech entrepreneur. And the risk/reward ratio changes with almost every shot; the last hole tends to be more fraught than the first in a competitive situation.

Part of the secret of playing good golf lies in understanding your own risk/reward predilections and developing a plan of attack that suits your personality and your game. If you tend to be conservative and get nervous when faced with tough, daring shots, you don't want a plan that calls for lots of forced carries or heroic routes to the hole. If your course has a few holes that always give you trouble, figure out a way to play them safely (such as taking three swings to reach a par-4 green, or four to get home on that long par 5). You want to chart the *easiest* way around a course, even if that means laying up here or skirting trouble there. Far better to plan for the occasional bogey instead of suffering many doubles or worse.

"Managing the course is extremely important, and taking risks is part of the game," says Gary Player. "But you need to make smart decisions. Play your game and take risks when it makes sense for your game. If you can't hit a cut shot, then play for the middle of the green and take your chances with your putter. If you try and hit a shot that you don't have in your bag, you will end up with a double instead of a par."

Jerry Woodard, a 40-year veteran caddie on the PGA and LPGA Tours, recalls a time when he and his player, Juli Inkster, were facing a yellow-light situation. "I told her we should play it safe, lay it up," Woodard recalls. "She snorted, said, 'Strap it on, Jer, we're going for it,' and hit the shot on the green. I learned early that you don't suggest anything to the pros unless they ask. Especially the women!"

"When we're in the go/no-go zone, I tend to think about the shot that happened just prior and the shot that will happen as a result," says Mike Danaher, a longtime caddie at the Beverly Country Club in Chicago. "If my golfer had a really good shot to get them to this point, they have good positive energy and can be more aggressive. If they made a poor shot and are in this situation, I would caution them to play it safe and just get back in the fairway. Also, if an aggressive shot has the potential to make the next shot very difficult, I would caution them on that as well. There's nothing worse than trying to be aggressive to save one stroke and costing yourself two."

"Confidence is the main factor when assessing a yellow situation," says Mike Maher, another experienced looper at the Beverly Country Club. "A caddie should never force a golfer to attempt a golf shot they don't feel is within their comfort zone. A major factor is determining the format of play. For example, whether it is a match or stroke play will play into the decisions to play aggressively or safe. When it comes down to it, a player's confidence needs to align properly with the strategy."

Lorne LeBere, known as "White Rabbit" during his long years on Tour, liked to get mathematical. "First thing you do is figure the odds," he says. "If it's 75–25 in my favor, we go. The pros like to go even when it's 50–50. They shoot at the flag, gamble, don't like to lay up . . . some you don't even *try* to talk them out of!"

The caddie's main goal is to make sure his player is comfortable and confident over the shot he's about to play. Play green-light golf the same way and watch your scores come down.

LPGA pro Andrea Knox successfully blasts the ball out of the trap at Black Diamond Ranch.

Play Sense-sational Golf

What's Your Dominant Sense?

Almost every golf instructor, from the Tour gurus to the local club pros, will tell you to "visualize" your shot before you hit it. Jack Nicklaus, as just one example, often said that he never pulled a club until he could picture the shot he wanted to hit "in his mind's eye."

That's all well and good, but these instructors don't often tell you *how* to visualize a shot. For some golfers, this bit of advice is worthless, since not all of us *have* a mind's eye.

Research by educators and others studying how we learn and assimilate information has shown that each of us tends to have a "dominant" sense; that is, one of our five senses takes a leading role in both how we absorb new information and, especially, how we utilize that information in repetitive tasks, such as swinging a golf club.

While the majority of humans tends to be visually dominant — they have that "mind's eye" that allows them to form the mental pictures that Nicklaus is talking about — many others are not. Visually dominant people have little TV screens in their mind that can create and play brief movies of what they want to happen.

It turns out that another subset of golfers is *kinetically* dominant. These golfers don't get a *visual* picture of a shot; rather, they get a specific kinetic *feeling* somewhere in their body just before they hit a good shot. Some get a warm, relaxed sensation in their hands, forearms, shoulders, back, torso, or legs that becomes their mental trigger, or "go" signal. When they get that special feeling, they know they're about to hit a good shot; when it's missing, something feels wrong and the shot often goes awry.

Another subset of golfers is led by their sense of hearing, or the *auditory* sense. For these players, golf is like a dance, played to an inner rhythm, a music only they can hear. For these players, the best results occur when they can feel an inner tempo that produces a smooth, balanced swing. Auditory-dominant golfers tend to be musically inclined. They often whistle or hum when they're playing well and in tune with that inner rhythm. Instead of trying to visualize a shot with a mental picture, these golfers try to sense the correct rhythm and tempo for the shot at hand. Watch the old instructional tapes made by Bobby Jones in the 1930s and you'll see that from address to follow-through, you could almost set his graceful, flowing swing to music. (There may be golfers dominated by their sense of taste or smell, but so far they haven't come forward!)

It shouldn't be too hard to figure out your dominant sense. The secret is to utilize that sensory ability in your golf game. If you are a visual golfer who can mentally "picture" the shot, don't stop there. In your mind's eye, envision the target as a bright, glowing, neon, Day-Glo bull's-eye. Don't just "see" the ball flying through the air, but envision that path as a bright and bold highway, rising and falling on its way to the destination. On the green, see your ball rolling through a bright plastic tube all the way into the hole. For you visual golfers, a good shot is one that follows the path your mind created for it.

If you are a kinetic golfer, you need to learn how to evoke your particular physical feeling or sensation before every shot. Take a moment to loosen, or lightly massage, whatever body part is the kinetic trigger, to elicit that feeling. Just remember to keep the target in mind, so the brain understands where you want the ball to go. For these golfers, that good feeling, somewhere in the body, results in good shots.

If you are an auditory golfer, you will always try to play with rhythm and tempo above all. You rehearse your swing, while thinking of the target, to get the right tempo for the shot and then simply launch into your particular golf dance. When you hit a good shot, someone watching will often say "good swing," because they have observed a swing that was rhythmic, unhurried, relaxed, well timed. The result will often be good, too.

Pay attention to your sensory controls, learn how to use them effectively for every shot, and you will begin to notice excellent results on the golf course.

The visually dominant Jack Nicklaus mentally pictured each shot before he hit it.

The Worst Lie of the Week

Keegan Bradley at the 2011 PGA Championship

The look on Keegan Bradley's face as he watched his chip shot run across the green of the 15th hole at the Atlanta Athletic Club was interesting — a combination of horror-struck and accepting. Horror-struck because his chip shot ran all the way across the green, passed the hole, and kept rolling until it dropped into the greenside pond beyond the hole. Accepting, because he knew before he hit that shot that there was a good chance it faced a watery death.

Of course, it was the last round of the 2011 PGA Championship at the Atlanta Athletic Club, and Bradley, a Tour rookie playing in the first major tournament in his career, was just one shot out of the lead when he stood on the 15th tee. But by the time he left the green, with a triple-bogey 6, he trailed the leader, Jason Dufner, by five shots, and his hopes for victory seemed dashed.

Steve "Pepsi" Hale, Bradley's caddie, had taken one look at the lie when he and Keegan arrived at the par-3 green, and he knew the next shot was going to be difficult. "He had hit a good shot from the tee," Hale says, "but the green was hard and fast, and the ball just took a bad bounce, went over the green, and into the rough. Horrible lie. It was easily the worst lie of the week. Ball was sitting down, way down. Maybe one chance in 50 that he could get any club on it, any control. We talked it over before the shot, and we decided he would aim off a bit, away from the hole, over to the left, where there was a slight rise or backboard. We hoped that might take some speed off any shot that came out hot."

It didn't. Bradley had to make a strong enough swing at the ball to get it out of the diabolical lie and onto the green, but he knew that there wasn't much chance of

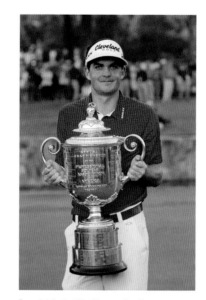

From triple to title: Keegan Bradley hoists the Wannamaker Trophy after winning the 2011 PGA Championship.

getting any spin to control the ball. He knew that the chances were it would come out hot and running. Which it did, zipping across the fast green and plopping into the water.

Keegan Bradley scrambled to make his triple-bogey 6 and fell five shots behind the leader, Jason Dufner, with three holes left to play. And Dufner, playing in the last group of the day, was standing on the tee box on 15, watching the whole thing unfold.

"You know," Hale said, "I believe that making triple on that hole is what won us the tournament. As a caddie, you learn to read your player's body language, so you know when you have to pick him up a little. I didn't have to do anything. He marched to the 16th tee. He was calm, determined, ready to play. He did it all himself, got himself back, and prepared to finish as best he could."

Bradley said later, "I just kept telling myself, 'Don't let that hole define this whole tournament.' Looking back, I don't know how else I could have hit that shot. It was just a bad lie."

Moving on, Bradley birdied the 16th. Then he canned a 35-foot putt on the 17th for another birdie. Finally, he parred the long and difficult closing hole. Then he waited for Dufner, who stumbled on the way in, leading to a tie between the two and a three-hole playoff. Bradley birdied the first playoff hole, Dufner bogied the second, and Bradley went on to win his first major title.

But the shot that Hale remembers most from the weekend was Bradley's drive on the last hole of the playoff. The 18th had been extremely difficult all week, with water down the left side and in front of the green, and a series of bunkers protecting the right.

"He had hit his 2-iron hybrid on that hole all week, and that's what he used for that last tee shot," Hale says. "Man, he striped that thing right down the middle . . . best shot he hit all week."

With his win at the PGA Championship, Keegan Bradley became only the third golfer in history to win a major in his first attempt, along with Francis Ouimet (1913 U.S. Open) and Ben Curtis (2003 British Open).

In doing so, he showed that even after a shot goes horribly wrong, you simply drop another ball, select the best target, and keep trying. Or as Winston Churchill memorably said, "Never, never, never, never give up."

The Chip Shot Heard 'Round the World

Hometown Boy Larry Mize Turns the Impossible into the Improbable

In 1986, Greg Norman had held the lead going into the final round of all four major championships. But he only managed to win one, at the British Open at Turnberry. And at the last of the four, he had been blindsided by the miraculous bunker shot on the last hole by Bob Tway (see sidebar, Inside Golf's Toughest Shots, p. 102).

But at the first major of 1987, the Masters at Augusta National Golf Club, Norman was again near the lead going into the last round on Sunday. Leading the tournament were Ben Crenshaw and Roger Maltbie, a stroke ahead of Norman and Bernhard Langer, and two shots in front of Larry Mize, a hometown boy from Augusta, Georgia, with just one win at the age of 28, and the dashing Spaniard Seve Ballesteros.

By the time the dramatics of the last nine on Sunday had played out, three players were tied for the lead: Greg Norman and Seve Ballesteros had each birdied the 17th hole to get to three-under par, one of the highest final totals in some time. And Larry Mize birdied the last hole to tie the two world-famous stars for the lead.

The three golfers headed for the 10th tee for the sudden-death playoff. All three played the par 4 in regulation, but Ballesteros missed a six-footer for par and trudged sadly back up the hill toward the clubhouse with his brother and caddie.

Norman and Mize moved to the difficult par-4 11th. Both hit the fairway with their tee shots. Norman put his approach shot on the right edge of the green, about hole high, but still some 30 feet across the slick green from the hole.

Mize was perhaps mindful of Ben Hogan's strategy for the hole. ("If you ever see me on the green at 11," Hogan had said, "You'll know I missed the shot." He explained that because of the little pond that lurks on the front left of the green, and the slope of the terrain from right to left, trying to get to that well-protected Sunday pin position on the left of the green is a fool's errand.) In any case, Mize's approach went wide to the right, almost all the way over onto the 12th tee box. He was left with a nasty little chip of some 140 feet. After a slight uphill rise to the edge of the green, his ball would then start rolling downhill across the green. Once it got rolling, there was nothing to help it stop, except for that dark little lagoon on the far side.

Mize and his caddie, Scott Steele, looked at the shot carefully. "I never consciously thought about making it," Mize recalled years later. "Our goal for the shot was to just try and get it close enough to make a par, and sort of put the pressure back on Greg. I mean, making it is always in the back of your mind, but I really just wanted to get it close somehow."

The strategy: hit a solid chip shot and hope for the best.

He pulled out his 60-degree sand wedge, collected his nerve and struck the shot. The ball popped forward, bounced twice up the hill and once more onto the green and rolled down the green with perfect speed, finally dropping gently into the cup.

Augusta, Georgia, native Larry Mize broke Greg Norman's heart (again) with his chip-in at the 1987 Masters.

"I couldn't believe it," Mize said. "I went a little crazy, running around screaming. I threw my club up in the air somewhere and knocked off my visor. I remember asking Scottie later, 'Where's the club?' Had no idea where it went! I finally calmed down and helped quiet the crowd a bit so Greg could putt."

Norman missed, and the green jacket belonged to Larry Mize. Adding to the excitement of the day, Mize received his winner's green blazer from the 1986 Masters champ and his boyhood hero, Jack Nicklaus.

As television announcer Steve Melnyk intoned, "Words do not do justice to the greatness of that shot."

CHAPTER THREE

Situational Thinking: Strategize Your Solution to Golf's Trouble Situations

From the first tee to the final putt, golf is an adventure. A round of golf can be a series of good shots, as well as not-so-good and even terrible ones; lucky bounces followed by unfortunate lies; short putts that miss and long bombs across the green that somehow manage to fall into the cup. If you are thinking like a caddie, you have preplanned your round, drawing up a strategy for playing each hole. If you are like most golfers, that plan can, and usually does, go horribly awry at times, and you can find yourself in some truly unexpected and unforeseen places.

But that's the game of golf. You take all the good shots and all the bad ones as they come, and at the end of the round you add them all up and see how you did. It's a game that should be played with equanimity and humor, and the acceptance that both good and bad shots can often be attributed to luck and human frailty. And it should be remembered that golf is just a game to be *played*, with a childlike sense of joy and wonder, and not something that defines one's worthiness as a human being. If even the top-ranked players in the world mess up from time to time, and they do, why do you expect anything close to golfing perfection from yourself?

In fact, watch what happens next time you see a Tour golfer hit a bad shot on TV. They might look aggrieved, mutter an imprecation or two under their breath, or outwardly display some anger and disappointment . . . but only for a moment. Usually the TV cameras cut away to a commercial so we don't see the player while he finishes blowing off steam, which often happens while he walks to his next shot. By the time the cameras come back from the commercial, the player is almost always under control again, calmly assessing his lie and situation, listening to the caddie reel off the yardage and the wind data, and planning the best way to make the next shot. Rarely, if ever, will a Tour player allow his

DEALING WITH ANGER AFTER A BAD SHOT

When the round is not going well, there's a place for some anger or at least irritation. But that's just for the player. Depending on his personality type, he can get steamed up and put those feelings to use. Obviously, it's got to be controlled and under the surface. And both the caddie and the player have to know if he is ticked off at himself or at the kind of results he's getting, based on the rub of the green. The caddie will react a little differently in each case. If the player is angry with himself, you let him use the energy of it, but everything you say is positive – about how the next shot is going to be right on target. If it's anger at a bad result from a good shot, you have to make sure that doesn't feed into an overall feeling that this isn't our day. Again, the idea is that the odds are going in your favor now – and the good swings or good putts are going to have to bring good results because the law of averages is on your side.

– Bobby Brown
PGA Tour Caddie

Opposite page: PGA Tour star Zach Johnson considers a two-putt strategy for a long putt.

How he got here doesn't matter: Keegan Bradley concentrates only on the next shot – his putt.

anger to carry over to the next shot.

Getting mad at yourself is certainly permitted. Because the golf ball is just sitting there, sometimes even on a tee, all golf errors are "unforced," or caused for the most part only by ourselves. So if you want to curse at yourself for hitting the ball in the woods or the sand or the water or the rough . . . go ahead! But give yourself a time limit on the self-hate: just enough time to walk back to your golf cart, or until you get within ten yards of the next shot. And then enforce the time limit; after it's over, forget the last shot and everything else except the next one.

Trying to play golf when you're still mad at yourself, or at someone else, is foolish. Anger is a strong inner emotion that usually causes muscle tension, mental anxiety, and self-doubt, all of which are usually fatal to the avowed goal of hitting each shot with calm confidence.

This chapter discusses some of the tough situational challenges that we all face from time to time on the golf course. But before you play any shot, and especially those that are tough and troublesome, you must first select a target for that shot and a strategy for getting to that target. If you play with a caddie, that's one of his main roles: to help you clearly determine where your next shot ought to go and how best to get it there, given your individual golfing prowess. Sometimes, as when the ball lies in the middle of the fairway, getting there is not a problem. Other times, as when the ball lies directly behind a tree or buried deep in the rough, you simply *can't* get there. So you and your caddie have to come up with a Plan B.

Because, unfortunately, most of us don't play with a caddie, devising those Plan B shots is all up to you. But when you play golf and think like a caddie, you get in the habit of thinking about each and every shot, from a 300-yard drive to a 30-inch putt, in terms of where are you going (target) and how to get there (best club and best shot). This think-before-you-act habit is especially important when you're faced with a tough trouble shot — those yellow-light or red-light situations. This chapter will help you strategize your way out of troublesome situations by pointing out the problems each one presents and how best to determine the green-light shot you need to recover.

PRE-PLANNING FOR DISASTER

Every golf course is different and each presents its own particular kinds of problems to the player. The smart and prepared golfer, or one who has years of experience on a particular course, will know the kinds of trouble shots he or she is likely to face, and will have either practiced them or have had enough experience with them to know how to hit them.

- **Do you play on a course with lots of mature trees lining both sides of the fairway?** You will need to know how to hit a low running shot to get safely under the limbs and back on the short grass.

- **Do you play on a Pete Dye-designed course, with those vast "waste areas"?** You must know how to pick a ball out of a sandy lie.

- **Do you play on a seaside links course, with rolling and bumpy fairways and deep, sod-faced bunkers?** These courses require the utmost in knowledge about playing with odd lies and tough bunker shots.

- **Is your course typically windy?** Rehearsing knock-down shots with various clubs will come in handy.

- **Does your course have deep rough like the ones prepared for the U.S. Open?** It will really help to know when you might get a flier, or when you need to choose a club with more loft to escape.

If you play the same course most of the time, you likely know where the trouble spots are; indeed, you may have been there many times! So you probably know the kinds of trouble shots you're likely to be faced with during a round. But if you're going to play a new course, in a new part of the country, or make that once-in-a-lifetime journey to the Home of Golf and its windy links courses, then practicing some of the unfamiliar shots you're likely to face is always a good idea.

Week in and week out, the professionals on Tour play on nicely manicured courses with a minimum of rough and fast greens that are often receptive to shots that spin. But in the weeks before the Masters at Augusta National, they practice putting on linoleum to get ready for the lightning-quick greens; before the U.S. Open, they'll practice driving the ball straight and toss a few balls into the deepest rough they can find, knowing that any slightly missed shots that week could end up in the hay; and before heading over to the British Open, they'll spend some time hitting knock-downs to get the feel of keeping the ball controlled and under the wind.

While they do this, they and their caddies will play close attention to the results of these new swings. A 7-iron, played back in the stance and with a slightly closed face to keep it on a low trajectory under the wind, will likely travel farther, including the roll, than a normal, high-arching, high-spin shot. Player and caddie need to know these distances when the time comes to play one in a tournament or meaningful round.

And better players who know how to play a course with a strategic plan also know how to develop an efficient practice plan, with at least two-thirds of practice time going for shots of 100 yards and in. These short-game shots — chipping, pitching, sand play, and putting — represent at least 60 percent of one's score. You can miss every green in regulation and still shoot even par if you can get the ball up and down from anywhere. Banging drivers for hours on the practice tee might be good stress-reducing therapy and great fun, but since you only hit, on average, 14 drivers per round, it's wasted time. On the other hand, if you two-putt every green,

Caddie Chad Reynolds shows the target to his man, Nick Watney.

that will account for 36 strokes in your round. So which club *really* needs to be your friend?

This may all seem like overkill, especially to the casual golfer, but if the goal is to hit nothing but green-light shots during a round, it makes sense to become familiar with the shots one is likely to face during that round. It's difficult to stand over an unfamiliar shot and make a smooth, confident, green-light swing. Instead of beating drivers for hours on the practice range, take a wedge and a few balls over to the side of the range and hit a few shots out of the thick rough to see how both club and ball react in that situation. Likewise, spend some time in the practice bunker hitting a few buried-ball, "fried egg" shots as well as ordinary bunker shots, so that when and if those situations arise on the course, you'll feel relaxed, comfortable, and ready to handle the tough shots with confidence. That will result in both better shots and lower scores.

So let's start going through some of the toughest situations and the toughest shots in golf, and see how to approach, analyze, and overcome golf's toughest situational problems.

THE FIRST-TEE JITTERS

For many golfers, the first shot of the day is always the toughest. Especially when one is playing in a tournament or in a match that means something. Many of us can be calm and collected until it's time to put the ball on its peg and let it fly. Then, one's breathing becomes short, the mouth dries up, the hands get sweaty, the heartbeat races, and the sudden realization that the game has begun hits like a ton of bricks. All of a sudden, all the trouble on that first hole . . . trees, water, bunkers, whatever . . . looms in your mind, and premonitions of disaster — balls lost or hit out-of-bounds, people laughing at you — fly into your head. It's almost as bad as having one of those nightmares where you're naked walking down Main Street!

Even if you're normally a good driver of the ball, those first-tee nerves can be jangling and scary. Things tend to speed up when the tension rises, including your swing and your thought process, and it's very easy to forget your game plan, your strategy, and your tempo, all in the name of trying to get the whole thing over with as fast as possible.

Caddies we talked to have basically two recommended approaches for first-tee nerves: 1) try to put them out of your mind or 2) face them head-on.

Relax and Forget It

This school of thought uses various techniques for first-tee relaxation, including:

1. Deep breathing. Yoga exercises always start with a few deep, "cleansing" breaths. This ancient and very simple technique focuses on making sure your body has enough oxygen so that

Spaniard Sergio Garcia has dealt with first-tee tension many times in his career.

your mind can think clearly and your body can release tension and stress along with the outgoing air from your lungs. The great Gary Player began his breathing exercises on the practice tee while warming up. "I did deep breathing and meditation on the range before going to the first tee, which is important. There are too many distractions on the first tee, so you need to get yourself in the right frame of mind before you get there," Player says. "That and positive thinking always worked for me."

2. **Clear the mind.** When the nerves hit, the mind becomes hyperactive, thinking about all the terrible things that can go wrong with the first-tee ball, and all the awful places the ball can end up. Caddie J. P. Wynne says, "I believe the best technique is to clear your mind of anything else going on in your life and think about the game . . . after all, most of this game is mental."

3. **Visualization.** Club caddie Mike Danaher likes his players to take a few deep breaths and then visualize the shot they want to hit. "Deep breaths and a vision of the perfect drive would be my recommendations," he says. "Picture the ball going right where you want it to and forget everything else." (See sidebar, Play *Sense*-sational Golf, p. 36.)

4. **Gear it down a notch.** Club caddie Mike Maher likes breathing and visualization, and he adds one more idea to the mix: gear it down and don't try too hard. "The first tee is a point of concern for many players," he says. "Perhaps the best approach is to take a deep breath, identify a realistic target, and try to swing the club at 80 percent of your normal speed. Many times golfers are filled with adrenaline on the first tee. Their grip gets tighter and their swing gets too fast. A calm approach, especially if there's a gallery, is best."

5. **Rehearse the first shot.** Longtime Tour caddie Montana Thompson believes one should rehearse that first shot of the day on the practice range before the round, and take the memory of

a good shot to the tee. "For most Tour players, it's an hour warm-up, with stretching, hitting balls, and putting," he says. "Many go through the entire course planning their shots on each hole as they warm up. At least visualize the first tee shot you are going to play and make it happen on the range. Take that visual to the tee. Let your instincts take over."

6. Laugh a little. Laughter is an excellent stress and tension reducer. Van Costa wrote a book, *What Club Shall I Hit?*, describing his years of caddying on the LPGA and PGA Tours, and tells a funny story about the time he was working for Mary Mills at the U.S. Women's Open. To help combat her nerves, she asked Costa to tell her a dirty joke after every birdie, before they went to the next tee. Then she went on a birdie run, and Costa began to run out of his supply of off-color jokes. After two birdies in a row, Mills then holed out for an eagle and waited expectantly for her caddie to deliver the goods. "I was tapped out and couldn't think of anything," Costa writes. "I called her over and whispered the most disgusting and dirtiest thought I could. Mary turned bright red and I was a little embarrassed. As she stood over [her tee shot] she backed off. She burst out laughing and couldn't stop. She addressed the ball again and the same thing happened. She was cracking up laughing on the fifteenth hole of the U.S. Open and couldn't stop! She was so loose by this time that she split the middle of the fairway, something she had not done on that hole all week."

EMBRACE THE MOMENT

The other caddie school of thought on first-tee nerves is that they are something to be embraced as proof positive that you're involved in a meaningful game of golf. In other words, first-tee nerves aren't *bad*, but something to welcome and even enjoy!

When the Plan Goes Awry

The day Annika Sorenstam went for it . . . and lost

Having already won the Kraft Nabisco and the LPGA Championships in the summer of 2005, Sweden's Annika Sorenstam came to the U.S. Women's Open, played at Denver's Cherry Hills Country Club, full of confidence about winning what the media was calling the Women's Slam — trying to win all four women's major tournaments in the same calendar year.

And in the thin air of Denver, she and her caddie, PCA Caddie Hall of Famer Terry McNamara, had developed what they thought was the perfect strategy for the week: leave the driver in the bag. Although Annika was among the LPGA's leaders in fairways hit, she decided to use her 3-wood from the tee all week, depending on her usual consistency to find the fairways, and the altitude to make up for any loss of distance.

It was a great plan, except it didn't work. And so on Sunday, for the final round, trailing the leaders by seven shots, she decided she had to try something different. So, on the first tee, out came the big stick. She hit it right, into a tree, where her ball ricocheted into a creek. On the 2nd hole, she drove into the U.S. Open rough and made another bogey. By the end of the first nine, she was 9 over for the tournament and out of the chase. (South Korean Birdie Kim sank a bunker shot on the 18th hole to win that year).

McNamara said that the strategy had been to leave the driver in the bag all week, except for some rare circumstances. But when she came to the final round several strokes behind, she decided she had to try to be more aggressive. "It didn't work," she said after the round. "In fact, it totally backfired."

McNamara agrees. "Hitting a driver on some of those holes was like trying to hit the ball into a thimble," he says. "We found out that it didn't work. But I guess we had to try something."

Annika was somewhat philosophical about the tournament. "It was just one of those weeks," she said. "Nothing happened. To win a championship like this you need some good momentum, and I just tried to find it. I have no idea where it is."

That's golf in a nutshell: good strategy plus good shots equals a win. Good strategy plus bad luck equals waiting for things to change down the road.

LPGA Hall of Famer Annika Sorenstam and her caddie, Terry McNamara, know how to master golf's toughest shots as a team.

Hall of Fame caddie Jerry Woodard, who caddied on the LPGA Tour for nearly 40 years, explains:

"I used to tell the younger players, when they confessed that they were nervous before teeing off on the 1st hole, 'You're *supposed* to feel that way!' Once, I had the bag of Sarah Lee, a young South Korean player, and she was terribly nervous before the start of every round. I finally took her over to talk to Patty Sheehan, who by then had won every big tournament in the book. And Patty told her that she always got butterflies before each round, too. 'I was sick to my stomach when I teed off for my first win, and I was sick to my stomach when I teed off for my 30th win,' Patty told her.

"It's just nervous energy," Woodard says. "You've got to feel that way before a match, embrace those jitters. They're there for a reason!"

And sometimes the jitters don't go away after that first shot, either. Hall of Fame caddie Lorne "White Rabbit" LeBere has looped for players who "were so nervous, they couldn't put the ball on the tee! Some guys take two or three holes to calm down and settle in," he says. "You just gotta try and get their minds off the situation at hand. Tell 'em a few jokes, talk about sports . . . anything!"

Whether you use a yoga-like deep breath or two, tell yourself a joke, or decide to embrace the jangling nerves as a good sign of competition, it's important to make sure you're still in control before you hit that first shot. Identify, visualize, and concentrate on the *target*, not the *situation*. Remind yourself to take it especially slow. It's a green-light shot — the ball's on a tee and the fairway awaits. Take a final deep breath, focus on the target, and make that aggressive shot to the target.

THE ROUGH STUFF

When you hit your ball in the fairway, life is good. Generally speaking, the fairway means a green-light shot. The ball sitting up atop grass that has been carefully mowed every morning to a height of about a half inch means that you can swing freely at it, make direct club-to-ball contact that imparts backspin for control when it lands, and even make the ball draw or fade as needed.

But when the ball comes to rest in the tall grass — even just an inch or two in length — it creates all kinds of problems for the golfer, in terms of strategy, distance control, spin control, and even making any kind of good contact.

The first thing caddies do, after finding a ball in the rough, is to examine the lie. "The lie determines the shot," says Hall of Fame caddie Alfred "Rabbit" Dyer. It doesn't matter if the ball is 50 or 500 yards from the target; the question should be: "Can I get a club on the ball?" More precisely, can you get the clubface on the ball without any grass between the two?

When the ball is in the rough, all kinds of things can happen that may affect the next shot.

Deep grass. A ball sitting down in several inches of grass is almost impossible to hit with any kind of control. First, depending on how thick and deep the grass is, it can be difficult just to make contact between the club and ball. Then, the tall blades of grass often grab the shaft and hosel of the club as you swing, flipping the toe over, resulting in a closed-face snap hook or pull to the left. Even if you can manage to propel the ball in the general direction you want, it will likely have no spin, resulting in a flier. (See sidebar, All About Fliers, p. 54.)

If your ball is so far down in the thick stuff that you had to step on it to find it, it may well be a red-light situation. Remember that you are always allowed to declare an unplayable lie, take a penalty stroke, and drop the ball in a cleaner place. (See Chapter Five, The

All About Fliers

A Matter of Physics

Despite the best efforts of club manufacturers to provide us with irons that boast sharp-edged grooves designed to eliminate the old-fashioned flier, they still occur. It's a matter of physics.

When a golfer hits a golf ball with his iron clubs from the fairway or any good lie, the ball climbs up the grooved face of the club as it is projected up into the air. The grooves impart backspin to the ball, which helps both the aerodynamic flight capabilities of the ball, and the ability to stop the ball when it lands on the green.

But when a ball nestled down into the rough is struck, the blades of grass get caught between the ball and clubface. This can reduce or eliminate the backspin imparted to the ball at impact. The result is a ball that comes out like a knuckleball. Without any of the aerodynamic control of backspin, the ball can shoot through the air like a rocket, overshooting the target by ten or 20 yards or more. Plus, when it does hit the ground, the lack of backspin means the ball will run and run until gravity ends its forward momentum. The combination of the knuckleball flight and lack of stopping spin means that fliers are almost impossible to control.

Any time you find your ball in the rough, look carefully at the lie. If there is grass behind the ball, the chances for a flier are excellent. You can play for a flier by taking a club with more loft (e.g., hit the 7-iron instead of the 6) to allow for the extra flight and roll. If the way to the green is open, you can play the shot to land in front and roll onto the putting surface. But if you need to land the ball on the green, because of hazards guarding the entrance, be mindful of what lies behind the green; fliers don't stop quickly. Australian Greg Norman recalled that in the 1980 Australian Open, playing the par-5 17th hole, he hit his drive in the rough and decided to take a 5-iron and lay up in front of the green, some 260 yards away. But his smooth swing and the flier lie sent the ball careening. It flew the green and kept going on the far side — he had a full wedge shot back. He later calculated that his smooth 5-iron went more than 300 yards!

That's the problem with playing from the rough: you never really know where the ball is going to go, and that lack of control can be frustrating. Give yourself the widest possible margin of error, play for an open landing spot, keep a firm grip, and hope for the best!

As longtime champion Gary Player knows all too well, controlling the ball out of the rough and sand can be difficult.

Rules to Live By) It may turn out that the only green-light play you have in such a situation is to take the sand wedge and pop the ball back onto the fairway. The weighted flange on a sand wedge will help the club cut through thick grass, and the club's high loft will help propel the ball up and out, although usually not very far. Remember, it's difficult to know for certain how the ball will come out of a deep buried lie; sometimes, despite all visual evidence to the contrary, the ball will shoot out of the rough like a scalded cat. Other times, the grass may grab the club, and the ball moves just a foot or two. Your previous experience in these rough conditions will help you estimate what might happen. But you never really know until you swing the club.

When trying to escape from thick rough, remember to grip the club a little firmer to help prevent the hosel-grab pull hook. It may sound counterintuitive, but another good method for escaping from a ball nestled down in the tall grass is to lower one's hands a bit at address to raise the toe of the club, and try to make the entire width of the clubface sweep through the grass. This helps counteract the tendency of the toe to flip over, and you'll find that the club, as it's designed to do, will often sweep through all but the thickest rough and make contact with the ball. It's still difficult to control the trajectory and distance of the ball coming out of the rough, but this method generally succeeds in propelling the ball forward and toward the target.

Medium-length grass. There are any number of possible lies to be found when the ball ends up in the primary rough — up to about two inches in height. Depending on the type of grass on the course and the time of year, you can get relatively good lies, where the ball sits atop the grass, or bad ones, when the ball falls through the blades of grass that surround it.

The primary cut of rough is generally a yellow-light situation. As Alfred "Rabbit" Dyer says, the lie determines the shot. If the ball is sitting up nicely and you can get the clubface on it without any interference from the grass, you can often make a normal shot. But if the ball is down, either slightly or completely, you may have to chip it out with a lofted club, or plan for the spinless flight and roll of a flier.

Caddies know that the weather can affect how a ball will react when played from the rough. If it's damp or there has been rain in the last few days, the rough can be extra thick and "juicy," which makes getting a club through it even more difficult. Likewise, if there has been a heat wave with blazing sunshine, the blades of grass in the rough will likely be thinner and weaker, and different scenarios for escape may be available. The types of grass are also different: in northern regions, where bent and fescue are the normal grasses, the rough can be fairly thick, but still playable, whereas golf courses in the Sun Belt states will often be planted in heat-resistant Bermuda grass, with long rough that resembles steel wool.

Light rough. Balls that end up in the first cut of rough, that slightly fuzzy border along most fairways, can usually be played like a normal, fairway shot. With most of the ball showing above the tallest blades, one can usually get the clubface directly onto the ball, eliminating the chance of a flier and imparting the spin necessary to control the flight and stop of the ball. Most of the time, these situations will still be green light.

There is no scientific formula for judging the lie when one is in the rough. You have to rely on your past experience, what your eyes tell you, and sometimes even your gut feeling. Hall of Fame champion Gary Player remembers one tough shot he once faced from the rough, and what it was that gave him his green light to make a confident shot:

At the 1972 PGA Championship at Oakland Hills Country Club in Michigan, there were ten of us within two shots of each other on the last day, and I came to the 16th with a one-shot lead. I had just bogeyed 14 and 15, and I knew that if I bogeyed 16 I was more than likely going to lose the tournament. I pulled my drive into the right rough, and it landed behind a huge willow tree. I was angry with myself, and when I got to my ball I was concerned. I had worked hard to win, and I did not want to let it slip away. I started to walk off the yardage to the green, which I could not see from behind the willow tree, and then something funny happened. I saw a divot from a shot I had hit during a practice round and immediately knew what the yardage was and what shot I had to hit because I had hit it just a few days earlier. That strange-looking divot calmed my nerves, and boy did it help. I hit a perfect 9-iron to about three feet, and that birdie putt is what eventually gave me the win. Confidence comes from experience and belief in yourself, and sometimes from a weird-looking divot.

Hall of Fame caddie Alfred "Rabbit" Dyer says, "If you're in high grass, it's harder to shape a shot. Because the tall grass intervenes, you can't always hit your normal fade or draw. Take the easiest route out of trouble and don't overswing."

Jim Tanner, a longtime club caddie in the Northeast, goes back to the risk/reward calculation when advising his player what to do in the rough. "You need to assess the risks," he says. "Can you make the shot [you want to hit]? Is there a chance of putting it in the water or a bunker? Always remember, you don't want to make your situation any worse than it already is."

Chicago-area caddie J. P. Wynne tells his players to take it easy in the rough. "It seems like many players lunge at the ball and swing too hard out of the rough because they are fearful they will not be able to get the ball out," he says. "It may be better to take one or two extra clubs and take a normal and relaxed swing at the ball."

"Use the right club," urges caddie Mike Danaher. "A shorter iron is going to cut through the rough easier than a wood. Don't worry about distance, and just try to advance the ball to put yourself in a good position for the next shot."

"With today's grooves, chances are much better for success from the rough," says Lorne "White Rabbit" LeBere, a Hall of Fame caddie with years of experience on the Tours. "Check the grass and the lie . . . how much will the ball jump outta there? Some grasses, like the Memphis bluegrass, and other strains with thin blades, you tend to get more fliers. During a practice round, if you can, throw a couple of balls down in the rough and see how they come out."

NINETY PERCENT AIR

If you play your golf on a seaside links or the desert Southwest, you usually don't have to worry about trees that much. But play anywhere else, and you are likely to find your ball stuck behind a spreading chestnut or some other variety of tall, woody flora at some point in your golfing career. When that happens, one has but three choices in shots: go over, go around, or go under. OK, yes, you can sometimes go *through* as well, but trees, despite what everyone says, are NOT 90 percent air!

The late Payne Stewart rarely found himself in the trees, but knew how to get back on the short grass.

As in all problem shots, the lie will be the main determinant of the kind of recovery shot that is possible. If your ball is in the deep rough as well as behind a tree, your choices are more limited. To shape a ball around a tree, or even to try and hit it high or low, the player must be able to make clean contact between the clubface and ball. A ball sitting down in the rough, in a bunker, or resting on a thick layer of pine straw will be very difficult to control. Consider your situation to be yellow light or red light, and look for a safe way to escape back into play.

Noted Trees in Golf History

The Hinkle Tree and the Eisenhower Pine

The Hinkle Tree

You could call this the Case of the Tree That Wasn't There . . . Until It Was.

It was during the first round of the 1979 U.S. Open. There was a slight backup on the tee of the par-5 8th hole at the famed Inverness Club in Toledo, Ohio. That delay gave two competitors, Lon Hinkle and Juan "Chi Chi" Rodriguez, time to look around and think.

It was Hinkle who first saw a different route to the hole: instead of playing down the fairway like everyone else, he noticed that if he turned to the left and struck a shot down the adjoining 17th fairway, he might have a shorter distance to reach the 8th green. So, after first checking to make sure there were no local rules, he pulled out his 2-iron and smacked one down the 17th. He used the 2-iron again to reach the green and two-putted for a birdie. His playing partner that day, Chi Chi, did the same.

The U.S. Golf Association and its tournament officials were not amused. Frank "Sandy" Tatum, then the president of the USGA, got on the phone, and by the next morning a brand-new 15-foot Norway spruce had been planted to the left of the 8th tee, an attempt to block off the shortcut route down the 17th.

In the second round the next day, Chi Chi had the honor when the group arrived on the 8th tee. Using a scorecard pencil for a tall tee, Cheech slammed a driver up and over the new tree, and Hinkle did the same. This time, Hinkle only had a 6-iron into the green, which he birdied for the second day in a row. But Hinkle's concentration during the tournament was undermined by the constant media attention to his little strategic shortcut, and he ended the tournament 20 strokes behind the eventual winner, Hale Irwin.

While the Hinkle Tree is famous as an example of the one and only attempt to use an outside agent to toughen a course during a tournament, and while the tree still exists (and is today more than 30 feet high), its significance on the course has waned. The pro tees have been moved back on the 8th hole, more trees were planted after the tournament to separate the 8th and 17th holes, and the shortcut is no longer possible.

The Eisenhower Pine

The huge 150-foot loblolly pine with its spreading boughs guards the corner where the 17th fairway turns to the left and climbs toward the green at the famed Augusta National Golf Club, home of the annual Masters Tournament. Because of its height and width and position some 200 yards off the tee, players in the Masters must negotiate their way around the tree, usually by means of a nice controlled draw around the corner.

One player who could never quite get that strategy down was club member, former president of the United States, and former commander of the European Theater of Operations during World War II Dwight D. Eisenhower. The tree is called the Eisenhower Pine, or just Ike's Pine, because it seemed to be a magnet for the president's tee shot on the 17th. Eisenhower is said to have bonked a ball off that tree almost every time he played the course. And he played it a lot; Augusta National was one of his favorite places to go to escape Washington, D.C., and Clifford Roberts, his good friend and chief political fund-raiser, was the club's CEO.

It is said that Ike annually petitioned to have the tree cut down, but despite his pedigree and political power elsewhere, he couldn't persuade Roberts or his copresident, Bobby Jones, to take a chain saw to the thing. The Eisenhower Pine continues to claim victims. It was from beneath the limbs of the tree during the 2011 Masters that Tiger Woods had to improvise an escape shot, which led to further injuries to his knee and Achilles tendon, keeping him out of action for most of the rest of the year.

Jack Nicklaus managed to avoid the Eisenhower Pine while winning his six Green Jackets at the Masters.

Matt Kuchar knows how to work his ball right-to-left or left-to-right to get around tree trouble.

To get a ball over a tree, you have to make it jump up into the air. How do you do that? Simple: hit down. A steep, descending blow into the ball will send the ball flying upwards sharply off the face. How high? That depends, of course, on the loft of the club: a sand wedge will carry over a higher and closer tree than an 8-iron. A "descending blow" does not mean a hatchet-like attack on the surface of the earth! You still want to make a nicely rounded golf swing, just at an attack angle slightly more V-shaped than normal. Focus on keeping your shoulders level through the entire swing; the tendency to dip one's rear shoulder "under" the ball at impact to "help" it up in the air is a fatal mistake.

You can add loft to an iron shot by opening the clubface at address. Just remember that the ball will tend to curve from left to right. Likewise, for shots under a limb, decrease loft by closing the clubface down and playing the ball back a bit in the stance. Plan for the ball to hook a bit; the closed face will cause that sideways spin.

Going around an obstructionist tree is almost always a safer alternative. But that depends on how much "around" means! Professional golfers can bend a shot to the right or the left, a little or a lot, depending on what they need. Most amateurs can't call on those kinds of shots, except after ten tries on the practice range! Remember: every shot has to be a green-light shot, and if you can't be 100 percent confident that you can hit a shot with a gentle hook or a power fade, then you should not attempt it. The best shots are the simplest, and the simplest shot is one you know you can make.

Caddies will always consider their player's strong and weak points when developing a game plan for a course, and when faced with a situation on the course that presents options. If his player needs to play a certain kind of shot — such as a 3-iron with a ten-yard hook, or a softly faded eight, the caddie knows if his player "has" that shot. If the player can stand over that shot with confidence and swing with aggression, then it's a green-light shot. If not, find the next best shot that can be made confidently.

THE SAND MAN

For the professional player, hitting a ball into a bunker is sometimes a good strategy (see Billy Mayfair's decision at Valencia described on pages 23–24). That's because professionals have little or no fear about bunker shots. As golf gurus like to keep telling us, bunker shots are supposedly one of the easiest shots in golf. Heck, you don't even try to hit the golf ball, you just dislodge the sand behind and beneath it, and the sand throws the ball up and out and onto the green. Simple!

Except for the 99 percent of the rest of us, for whom an unanesthetized root canal would be preferable to facing a shot from the sand. We worry about the consistency of the sand. Too soft? Hit it harder. Too hard? Hit it softer. We fret about exactly how much sand we're supposed to displace in the bunker shot and either dig too deeply, resulting in a muffled swat that doesn't get the ball out (which means, oh God, we have to do this again!), or we flinch at the bottom of the swing, catch the ball cleanly without taking any sand, and send the ball rocketing over the green and into the great unknown that lies beyond.

Again, the main reason golf professionals are usually so comfortable and unafraid in a bunker is because of the amount of time they have spent in one — practicing, practicing, and then practicing some more. They spend hour after hour testing out all kinds of different lies — ball below feet, ball on side hill, ball sitting down in sand — in all kinds of sand conditions: hard, firm, silica-like, hard packed, wet, and dry. Plus, they pay thousands of dollars to their swing gurus to stand in the sand with them, offering instant professional feedback and advice. And, they can

PGA Tour star Luke Donald spends hour after hour practicing sand shots.

look forward to a half-hour massage afterwards in the clubhouse from their own personal traveling masseuse. It's little wonder, then, that the pros can play these shots with so much confidence. They know how to hit a bunker shot with spin that will drop on the green and stop short. They know how to hit one without spin, that lands softly on the green and rolls toward a distant hole. They know how to hit the high floater, the low runner, and everything in between.

Most of us don't have that same degree of confidence in the sand. Or much of *any* confidence in the sand. Because most of us only face a sand shot when we land in a bunker during a round. Many golf course practice ranges don't have a practice bunker, and even if they do, we're usually too busy having fun bashing drivers instead of practicing in the sand. It would behoove any golfer who wants to shoot lower scores to spend some time practicing this relatively easy shot; even better, to invest in a half hour of your golf professional's time to get some knowledgeable tips, swing thoughts, and feedback on this often-used and often-abused shot.

GREENSIDE BUNKERS

Remember, your inner caddie wants to insist that every shot you make is a green-light shot. If, when you see your ball is in a bunker, you begin hearing warning sirens and envision an entire corps of drum majorettes marching around the edge of the bunker waving their bright-red flags, getting to green is going to be tough. If nothing else, every golfer should be prepared to hit a simple, basic, green-light bunker shot, in which the operating strategy, first and foremost, is to get the ball out of the bunker. Once you've mastered the basics of the bunker shot, you can begin to add techniques that will help you not only extract the ball from the sand, but begin to control that shot and aim it more precisely toward the target.

In his golf schools, books, and articles, Dave Pelz, the guru of the short game, tries to first teach that basic get-out-of-the-sand shot. The technique is quite simple and stress free, and is a good place for most sandophobics to start. Buy one of his books or videos, or attend one of his short-game schools, to learn all the details. But here is the Pelz method, boiled down:

1. The swing. In a greenside bunker, take the club slowly back to a position where your arms are parallel to the ground, your wrists are fully cocked, and the club is pointing straight up, perpendicular to the ground. An observer would call it halfway back, as opposed to a full backswing. From that position, make a smooth, accelerating swing into the sand just behind the ball (concentrate on a single spot about two inches behind the ball — look for a tiny pebble or discolored grain of sand and keep your eyes focused there). Finally, don't stop swinging the club until you reach what Pelz calls the "world-class finish": hands up and over the front shoulder, arms fully extended, body turned to face the target. It's a basic halfway back, fully through swing. Do not try to swing harder or easier than normal — just swing the club halfway back, down, and through to the high finish.

Phil Mickelson's method: club displaces sand, sand throws ball into air.

65

2. Ball position. Pelz teaches a forward ball position from the bunker. If, for a normal golf shot from the grass, one lines the ball up roughly with the heel of the front foot, in a bunker, make sure the ball is sitting an inch or two *forward* of the front foot as you take a stance. This will initially seem a bit awkward , because it forces the golfer to reach a little to make contact with the sand. But that reaching forward helps with the proper weight shift and encourages an accelerating swing.

3. Stance. Should be comfortable and normal. At address, place most of your weight on the front foot (left side for a right-handed golfer). Keep it there through the swing. Flare or open your front foot a bit to the left (again, for a rightie).

4. The club. While learning this basic escape shot, don't worry about opening the clubface. Keep the face square or maybe open just a bit (whatever feels most comfortable). The modern high-lofted sand wedge is designed, with its heavy and flanged bottom edge, to glide through the sand without digging in, as long as you keep the swing moving to its high finish. It will displace the sand beneath the ball and toss the ball up and out.

If you do this simple swing correctly, you will hear a satisfying *thump* as the club hits the sand, and the ball should float up and out onto the green. Once you've mastered the basics, you can begin to experiment and add more elements that will help you control the ball, the distance, and the spin.

If you're in a deep greenside bunker and need to get the ball up quickly to clear the front lip, you can add loft by opening the clubface. Turn the handle to the right and then grip it as for a normal shot. This adds several degrees of loft to your 58- or 60-degree sand wedge. Make the same basic swing described above, and the ball will come out higher. An open clubface will also send the ball a shorter distance in the air and will cause it to fly directionally off to the right of the line of the swing, so you'll have to make some adjustments in aiming and swing speed to compensate.

As you practice this shot, you will learn that playing the ball even further forward will result in a higher, softer pop-out. Playing it a bit back towards the center of your stance will result in a lower, faster-running shot. Once you've got the basics down pat, you've got a surefire, bunker-escaping, green-light shot in your repertoire. Then you can begin experimenting with longer backswings, more open clubfaces, and knees flexed (more or less). However, it's that simple basic shot — ball forward, weight forward, halfway back to full-finish swing — that will serve you well out on the course when you need to get the ball on the green.

FAIRWAY BUNKERS

When your ball ends up in a fairway bunker, the strategy is quite different than a shot played from a greenside bunker. Instead of just getting the ball onto the green, the golfer wants to try to advance the ball forward toward a distant target with a full swing. Again, the first rule is to get the ball back in play, or onto the grass.

From a fairway bunker, the goal is to hit the *ball first* and then the sand. It's a pick-it-clean kind of shot, as opposed to the explosion shot in a greenside bunker. Hitting the sand behind the ball first will result in a severe loss of distance and elevation, which can be fatal.

The first thing caddies look at when considering a fairway bunker shot is the lie. Is the ball sitting atop the sand, or has it wormed itself down into the sand? If it's the latter, then reach for a lofted club, like a wedge or 9-iron, and plan to just get it back into play. If there's a high lip at the front of the bunker that needs clearing, you've got to use a more lofted club. Trying to pick the ball cleanly out of the fairway sand often results in a lower flight trajectory as you catch the ball lower on the clubface. The smart caddie will factor that into his club recommendation.

A professional golfer, armed with experience and practice, can usually nip a ball out of a fairway bunker without difficulty, and still control the trajectory, spin, and distance. Amateurs and hackers just don't have the same degree of swing consistency or accuracy, and therefore must consider all the possibilities of a less-than-perfect shot. At the 2000 PGA Championship, Tiger Woods hit a 3-iron from a downhill lie in a fairway bunker 210 yards from the pin that hooked perfectly around a tree and landed on the elevated green some seven feet from the hole. He calls it one of the best shots he's ever hit in his life. You and I would probably be much better off hitting a 7-iron to about 100 yards in front of the green and then an easy wedge. We might not make the birdie that Tiger did on that hole, but we also probably wouldn't make a double-bogey or worse.

It's almost always a good idea to take an extra club from a fairway bunker, even if there aren't any hazards to clear in front of you. First, an extra club will compensate for the loss of distance in case you catch the ball a little heavy (that is, hit the sand first). Second, the fairway bunker shot calls for a quiet, inactive lower body, which reduces the power of this arms-only swing. Using more club compensates for that. Third, to help pick the ball cleanly out of the sand, it helps to choke up an inch or so on the handle, reducing the overall arc of the swing, which will also reduce the normal distance produced by the club. And finally, it's always a good idea to swing easily from a fairway bunker, with reduced effort and power. By taking an extra club, or sometimes two, you can relax, make a smooth, effortless pass at the ball, and let the club do the work.

Here's how it's done:

1. **The stance.** You do not want a lot of lateral-weight

movement on a shot like this. Think of it as an arms-only swing, keeping the lower body as anchored as possible. To help with this, widen your normal stance by a few inches — spread both feet out just a bit wider than you normally do. And don't dig your feet too far down into the sand; that will lower your swing arc and cause your clubface to bottom out lower in the sand — not what we want. Instead, try digging the inside edge of each foot in a little toward the center, creating a solid platform for the swing. Then, just try to keep everything from the waist down as quiet as possible throughout the swing: weight centered, and knees flexed and level.

2. The club. Choke up an inch or two on the handle. This will shallow the swing arc and help you pick the ball cleanly from its sandy lie. Play the ball in the center of your stance, or just a bit behind center — you want to hit into the back of the ball first and take as little sand as possible.

3. The swing. Armed with an extra club or two and swinging from a solid, unmoving lower-body base, make as smooth and relaxed a swing as you can. Trying to power a ball out of a fairway bunker will often result in a lunge or a slip or a lateral move into the ball, which will sharpen the angle of attack and make the club dig into the sand — not what we want. In addition to keeping the lower body quiet, keep your shoulders level throughout the swing — no "helping" (actually hurting) by dropping the rear shoulder down as you come into the ball. You want to feel like you're trying to top the ball in order to pick it clean.

Remember: Rule One is to get the ball out. If the lie is iffy — the ball sitting down or less than cleanly on the sand — or if the lip of the bunker is too high, don't try one of those miraculous Tiger Woods-like shots. If your target is guarded in front by hazards, sand, or deep grass, take enough club to safely clear the trouble, or else plan to lay up and recover with the next shot. You've got to consider the risk/reward ratios for this shot: As Tour caddie Lorne "White Rabbit" LeBere says, "If you're at least 75 percent confident you can make the shot, go for it. If not, take a safer route to the target."

FRIED EGGS AND OTHER PROBLEMS

One of the biggest problems with bunker shots is that the lie you get is often unusual, uncomfortable, or less than perfect. Hey, that's why they call them hazards! At least in our modern game, the tradition is to provide nicely raked bunkers with smooth surfaces. In the old days, you could end up in a footprint, next to a rock or a stick (which you couldn't move), or, in places like Oakmont in Pennsylvania, in a bunker with two-inch-deep furrows (they used weighted rakes to create them on purpose!). In addition, some bunkers can be shallow with low lips, and others can be deep. In Scotland, they tend to go for the deep kind, and they often build the fronts of the bunkers with layers of sod — the famous "revetted" bunkers. Think of that well-known "Road Hole" bunker on 17 at St. Andrews — it's small, filled with soft sand, and calls for a shot that has to clear at least six feet of sod to get out.

And the consistency of sand in a bunker varies from course to course, and sometimes even from hole to hole on a course. Some bunkers are filled with soft, fluffy, silica-like sand that resembles powdered sugar. Others feature more tightly compressed or packed sand. Wet sand, after a downpour, is entirely different from dry sand.

The good news is that your basic, get-out-of-jail sand shot, described above, should work in almost all conditions you encounter in a bunker. The only difference is that the ball may react differently coming out. A ball played from soft, light, dry sand tends to spin more than one played from heavy, wet sand. The latter tends to hit and roll more than the former. A ball played from an upslope tends to fly higher than one played from a downhill lie. Again, the latter shot will usually come out on a lower trajectory and roll more, as the downhill angle of attack delofts the club.

Here are some other bunker tips:

Slopes. The key in facing a bunker shot from either an uphill or downhill slope is to set your shoulders along the same line as the slope. On an uphill lie, make sure your front shoulder is higher than the back shoulder at address, on the same level as the slope of the hill. Do the reverse when playing a ball that rests on a downhill slope. Next, just make the same halfway-back, full-finish swing, keeping those shoulders on the same line as the hill throughout.

For a bunker shot from a sloping lie. set your shoulder level to match the slope and always finish with a complete follow-through as Luke Donald does here.

Ball above or below feet. Sometimes, your ball comes to rest in a bunker several inches higher than your feet at address. The only change to make from the normal bunker shot here is to choke up on the handle an inch or two (depending on the severity of the incline). The ball from this position has a tendency to come out left of the target, so adjust your aim accordingly.

When the ball is below your feet in the bunker, make sure you get down to it by flexing your knees to adjust. Then make your same bunker swing.

Fried eggs and buried lies. If the sand in the bunkers where you play is soft, a high-flying wedge approach shot that lands there may come to rest in the impression it makes when it hits. This is the "fried egg" lie, where the ball is the "yolk" and the circle

A GREAT BUNKER SHOT

I was caddying for Al Geiberger at the 1975 Ryder Cup Matches, played that year at Laurel Valley in Ligonier, Pennsylvania, and the U.S.A. won big, as it did often in those years before the European players were added to the other side. Al was paired against Bernard Gallacher in the Sunday singles, and the U.S. had already won the Cup. But the TV cameras were following our match closely, and Al found himself down by three with three holes to play. Somehow, he fought back to win the 16th and 17th. On the 18th, Gallacher hit his approach on the green. Al had a fairway wood and pulled it a bit, and the ball rolled into the front bunker. When we got to the ball, we saw it had just dribbled about six inches into the sand and stopped on a downhill slope. There was barely enough room behind the ball for Al to swing his club back, never mind the downhill lie. He took one look at the lie and said, "Geez." I'll never know how he did it, but he came out of that bunker, flew the ball 30 yards, and stopped it six feet from the hole. Gallacher three-putted and Al made his, so we halved the match. When asked why he tried so hard in a meaningless match, Al said, "It was for the good of the game."

— Van Costa
Former Tour caddie and
PCA Caddie Hall of Famer

of sand displaced by the ball hitting and sticking is the "white." This makes it more difficult to hit a regular bunker shot, where you strike the sand two inches behind the ball, as that extra circle of sand will slow down the clubface as it plows through.

The solution is counterintuitive. One would think that the way to extricate a ball sitting down in the sand would be to open up the clubface and increase the loft. One would be wrong! Instead, close the clubface down and make a more chopping-like swing into the sand just behind the ball. For this shot, you want to bury the club in the sand with power, not worrying so much about making a full follow-through. When the club powers into the sand behind the ball, it will throw both sand and ball up and out. The ball will jump out and run like a scared rabbit, and there's not much you can do to control it. But it will come out, and that, remember, is your primary goal.

Occasionally, you get really unlucky and face a "plugged" lie, where the ball burrows down into the sand so that some or even all of it is beneath the surface of the sand. These are ugly to behold! Again, the solution is to close the clubface down and make a sharp, descending blow into the sand behind the ball, leaving the clubface in the sand or with just a minimum of follow-through. This will displace a great cloud of sand, in which the ball should pop out and begin to run across the green. There's not much you can do to control the distance, because you've got to slam the club into the sand to make sure the buried ball comes out, and the harder you swing, the more the ball will roll. Keep that in mind if there is trouble on the far side of the green.

Mike Maher, a longtime club caddie from Chicago, advises most golfers to concentrate on the first goal of a bunker shot: to get out. "Pros make bunker shots look easy because they practice them all the time," Maher says. "For the average amateur golfer and weekend warrior, it's best to focus on just getting the ball on the green. Too many times, players try to get cute with a flop shot from the sand and fail to get out of the bunker. You can't make a sand save if you're hitting two from the sand. Get it on the green and get the flat stick in your hand."

Longtime caddie at Pinehurst Willie McCrae has a quick solution to the problem of a ball buried in the sand: "With a buried lie, close the clubface," he says. "You always want to put sand on the green." That is, strike the sand firmly just behind the ball and try to dislodge as much sand as possible — the ball will come out with the gob of sand.

DON'T FORCE IT

Golf course architects love to scare the hell out of us. If there's a way they can throw something dangerous between us and our target, they will. From a cross-bunker to a yawning chasm, architects like to make us think twice, entice us to take the dangerous route (with the promise of a birdie, an easy putt, or some other reward for the risk), and hopefully make us think, just at the top of our backswings, "What the heck am I doing???"

And so there are holes that bend artfully around a water hazard, daring us to cut off as much as we think we can. There are innocent-looking bunkers or babbling brooks that seem to be located exactly where we want our ball to go. There are rocky waste areas or reflective ponds that don't seem to be in our way, until we realize that we must hit our ball over them in order to get to the Promised Land.

After shots like these, if successful, we have an easy shot or a birdie putt left. If unsuccessful, we have to fight to make a double- or triple-bogey.

The forced-carry shot is more mental than anything else. Consider probably the most famous forced-carry shot in golf: Pete Dye's 17th-hole island green par-3 at the The Stadium course

Sergio Garcia (right) and his caddie, Glenn Murray (left), watch the results of one of the Spaniard's escape shots.

at TPC Sawgrass. The professionals play this hole at about 135 yards. Put a tee and a green 135 yards apart in the middle of a field, and most players will be thinking, "I can make a one here." But surround that green with water (and add the pressures of the Player's Championship title, a national TV audience, and several thousand raucous fans surrounding the green), and it's a hole that the pros admit gets into their heads, starting at about the 10th tee.

The Stadium course's island-green hole is more than a forced-carry shot, of course. The player must not only hit the ball far enough to reach the green, but also hit it straight enough to land on the green, and not so far as to bounce over the green. It's Dye-abolical in four dimensions.

Most forced-carry shots only ask that we hit the ball far enough to clear the trouble that lies in front of us. And hitting a ball far enough is a simple matter of selecting the right club that will carry that distance, considering wind, lie, and other conditions that might affect the shot. But nothing in golf is a simple matter!

When the professionals and their caddies approach a forced-carry shot, one of the first data points that the caddie collects is the distance to the point which must be carried. For instance, on a par-3 hole with a water hazard in front, the caddie will find out the distance to the edge of the hazard *and* the distance to the actual target, the hole. The first number will help identify the shortest club that may be used for the shot, given all the other conditions that may be present, such as wind behind or in the face of the player. Once the must-carry number is identified, then the player and caddie can calculate the distance to the target and select the right club.

What must be conquered more than anything in this situation is the mental approach. A good caddie will look at each shot as a problem that must be solved — not as a continuum of shots that have been played, or in terms of what might, or might not, go wrong. A caddie will, as we've seen, check the lie, identify the target, calculate the distance to the target, consider any other salient influences, and come up with a club, or perhaps a choice of two clubs for the player to select. Whether or not the very Gates of Hell lie yawning in front of the target matters little to a caddie and his player. The target is the only thing that matters, as well as answering the question, *What's the easiest and best shot to get there?*

That is quite a bit different from the way most of us approach the forced-carry shot. We spend most of our time contemplating the hazard that lurks in front of us, and imagine all the different ways we can, or have, hit our ball directly into it. So we stand over our shot with all kinds of negative thoughts rushing through our heads: *Don't hit this one fat, or else! You hit one right in that lake last time! Omigod, if this one goes in that bunker, Fred will win the hole and I'm cooked.* Is it any wonder that, with those kinds of messages reverberating in one's thoughts, the brain will believe that what you're really trying to do is hit the ball *into* that very hazard . . . after all, that's all you're thinking about!

The key to this kind of shot, then, is to go back to basics: identify your target with precision, select the club and the shot that you *know* you can make (the green-light shot), and make an aggressive swing at that *target.* It should be the target you're thinking of, not the disaster that will ensue if you mess up.

The hazards that must be carried in these kinds of shots are more mental hazards than real ones. Do you think about the million blades of grass your ball must pass over on its way to the target on a normal shot? Of course not. So why let that creek, or arroyo, or deep bunker enter your thoughts at all? You're not going there, you're going over it to the target.

That is not to say, however, that you should just proceed as if the hazard doesn't exist. Obviously, when considering the shot to be made, and deciding the best and easiest way to play it, one has to take into consideration the risk/reward aspect of the shot. And if the greatest risk is that the ball might fall short into trouble, whether through a bad swing or an unlucky gust of wind, then it is reasonable and intelligent to take an extra club to make sure that doesn't happen.

If one is a normal 7-iron distance from the target, but a deep bunker lurks waiting to catch a ball that comes up a bit short, it is a smart play to choose a 6-iron and resolve to make a nice smooth swing with it. With the shorter club, there is always a tendency to swing a little harder, especially at the last second, to make doubly sure the ball gets to the target. That can often result in a disastrous outcome. With a longer club, there is little doubt that the ball will get there, so you can concentrate on making a controlled, easy pass at the ball. There will be no tension, no last-minute thought to swing from the heels, no fear — just the confidence that comes from knowing that you've got plenty of club to get the job done.

One year during the Ryder Cup matches, Stuart Dryden, the caddie for Northern Irishman Ronan Rafferty, had calculated the yardage for an approach shot at 180 yards, a perfect 6-iron for his man. Or so he thought. Rafferty took a look at the shot and the bunkers he had to carry in front of the green and said, "I like the 4." Dryden was momentarily shocked. "I had to have a think about this," he says. "If I come back with the 6-iron, he's going to be confused." Dryden looked at his green diagram and noted that there was a little room behind the flag, so he countered Rafferty by suggesting an easy 5-iron. "Plenty of club, you can commit to the shot," he told his man. Rafferty hit a good shot with the 5-iron and, sure enough, the ball went a bit long, just catching the back fringe of the green. When they arrived at the ball, Rafferty heaved a sigh of relief. "I don't know what I was thinking," he told his caddie. "That 4-iron would have landed in the hot dog stand!"

Many times, the forced carry is an exercise in hubris: you want to get home in two shots on a par-5 hole, but to do so requires an accurate 3-wood shot that will either bounce its way onto the green through a narrow opening between hazards, or will have to fly about 220 yards in the air — the kind of shot you manage to pull off about once in every ten attempts. Those are the red- or yellow-light shots that should be avoided, unless the circumstances of the match dictate that you must try. When the risk/reward odds are stacked against you, it's always advisable to select an easier shot, one that has a much better chance of success. A layup, chip, and two-putt par is always better than a heroic effort that ends up in the drink.

For club caddie Mike Danaher, forced carries are all about mind over matter: "Take an extra club, swing smoothly, and forget about the obstacle," he recommends. "Once you've decided to go over the water, forget the water is even there and just envision the ball landing safely on the other side."

Montana Thompson, longtime Tour caddie, thinks these kinds of shots boil down to the basics: get the correct yardage, don't guess, then trust the shot. "Billy Mayfair once asked me what was the most important piece of advice I could give to a player," Montana recalls. "My answer was simple: commit to the shot. Don't be standing over the ball and wonder if you've got the right club, think about where not to hit the shot, or allow any doubt or indecision to enter your mind. Pick the club and commit to the shot."

Lorne "White Rabbit" LeBere, who caddied for several decades on the Tours, always had a simple philosophy when it came to forced carries or other tough decisions: Limit the damage. "It's always better to make a bogey and go to the next hole," he says.

STORMY WEATHER

Nobody likes playing golf in bad weather, which is why most of the time we don't. But whether it's the weekly PGA or LPGA tournament, or your club's annual member-guest, sometimes the show must go on, even if it is pouring rain, or cold and windy, or something worse.

The first thing that should be adjusted for the weather is your attitude. You know before you tee off that it's going to be unpleasant out there, but it's going to be just as unpleasant for your opponents. If you can't talk your fellow competitors into doing a coin-flip for the match, then you just have to make up your mind that you are going to try your best no matter how cold or wet or miserable the conditions. Dress appropriately — layers for cold and rain gear for wet — and rustle up some extra towels, and pack additional golf gloves in the bag to replace the ones that are sure to get wet.

Caddies hate bad weather more than their players, because the conditions add extra duties to their job. Rule One is to keep the player as dry as possible, which means that he gets the umbrella. Rule One-A is to keep the player's clubs and especially the grips as dry as possible, which means using protective bag covers and trying to keep at least one towel dry to soak up the moisture. Only then does the caddie perform all his other tasks during the round.

But caddies also know that the weather affects and tests everyone's game. Distances may remain the same, but both player and ball suffer when it is wet and cold. In such conditions, the ball doesn't carry as far, and doesn't roll as far once it hits the turf. Both rough and bunkers become even more problematic in a soaking rain. The player's range of movement can be impeded by extra clothing and rain gear, wet grips and cold hands mean a loss of control, and it takes a lot of patience to perform well when the conditions are miserable. Caddie and player alike must make all kinds of adjustments: to their strategy, their decision making, and their club selections.

While it is always important to play the game one shot at a time, it's even more so when the conditions are vile. Each shot must be taken as a separate problem to be solved, and the conditions will play a huge part in identifying an appropriate target, selecting the right club, and even in making good putts on the green. Throw away the normal playbook, forget the usual yardage-to-club ratios, and plan to play each shot as best you can.

If you are riding in a cart with rain flaps, you can keep the clubs sheltered from the rain. You'll still need extra towels for hands and grips, and your umbrella for walking to and from your ball. In cold conditions, a pair of those cart gloves — oversized pull-on mittens — are invaluable in keeping your fingers from getting numb.

Playing in bad weather conditions requires patience and lots of it. It's easy to let the conditions get to you, which takes away from your concentration. It's OK to moan and groan while walking or riding between shots, or when standing around the tee or green waiting for your turn to play. But when it comes time to make a shot, you've got to ignore how wet and cold you may be, and think only about the shot.

In tough conditions, it's more important than ever to go through your Five-Finger Format checklist, plus:

Take a close look at your lie. Make sure the ball isn't sitting in a puddle. If it is, you are allowed to take a free drop at the nearest

Singer Michael Bolton knows that the weather conditions at Pebble Beach can affect his play. (Note: In tribute to caddies everywhere. Michael has recorded the stirring PCA anthem "Five Feet Away," available at www.PCAhq.com.)

point of (dry) relief. If water is visible when you step near your ball, you are allowed relief. You are also permitted to move the ball if your stance causes casual water to pool up from the turf around your feet. Unless absolutely necessary, don't try to play a shot from a soggy lie; the ball will often come out without spin when water gets between the clubface and ball, and if you hit even a little turf before hitting the ball, the moisture-filled grass will muffle the shot. You'll get a splat with no distance.

Allow for the conditions. When selecting your target and the club to get there, remember that a golf ball won't fly as far on a wet and cold day as it will on one that's dry and sunny. The heavy atmosphere will take some distance off every shot, not to mention whatever wind is blowing, so be sure to take an extra club for most shots. The ball also won't roll nearly as far when it lands on wet ground, so you've got to take that into consideration as well. It's almost impossible to overclub on wet and cold days, and even if you manage to overfly the target a little, the ball will usually hit and stick.

Swing easy. Ask any Scottish caddie about playing in strong wind. "When it's breezy, swing easy," is their favorite mantra. The same holds true if it's wet or cold. The key to making good shots in bad weather is to make solid contact between the clubface and the ball. Trying to overpower the ball is always a fatal mistake. Instead, take plenty of club for the shot you want to make, and try to make a slow, easy pass at the ball, swinging with less than full power. You will get far better results if you make solid contact between the ball and club than if you try to swing hard and miss slightly.

Allow for extra clothing. If it's cold, wear several layers. If it's raining, put your bulky rain gear on. In either case, your ability to make as full a turn and as fast a swing as on a hot, sunny day is going to be somewhat compromised. That will reduce your swing arc, lessen your swing speed, and reduce the distance your shot travels. Know this before selecting a club and plan for it.

It should be evident that your normal yardage book is mostly useless on a bad-weather day. A club that normally goes 150 yards on a bright and sunny day may only fly 125 yards in cold, wind, and rain. Don't be ashamed for needing two or even three more clubs on a shot; the challenge on bad days is to get around the course in as few strokes as possible. You can do this most effectively by taking more club than you think necessary and swinging easy. Play the ball back in your stance an inch or two and just go for good contact.

It is most important to play within yourself when the conditions turn nasty. Resolve to play every shot at about 75 percent of full power. Don't attempt any heroic shots on wet and cold days. Select the easiest green-light shot that's available. Making pars is great; making bogies is entirely acceptable. In fact, on wet and cold days, a bogey should be considered the "par" for a hole. Lower your expectations, play the game the conditions give you, and try to enjoy the experience. Some golfers are good "mudders" who relish the extra challenges of wet conditions. It makes golf on a bad day a game within a game, and some find that fun.

Jerry "Hobo" Osborne, a longtime Tour caddie, believes in keeping it simple when the weather turns bad. "Preparation is the key," he says. "Have extra towels. In cold weather, keep your golf balls in your pocket to keep them warmer."

Four of the Toughest Bunker Shots and How to Hit Them

Secrets You Should Know

Not every bunker shot provides you with a nice, clean lie from the bottom of the bunker. By their nature, bunkers can be tricky to negotiate, especially when your ball lands in an awkward position in or near the sand. Here are four of the toughest bunker situations, and what you should remember about getting out.

Ball outside bunker, feet inside. Depending on the depth of the bunker, this shot can range from mildly troubling to near impossible! Most of the time, you'll have to hit the ball with a baseball-like swing. These are almost always yellow-light situations, which means forget going for the green, and select a target that you can reach with an abbreviated, punch-out shot.

- Choke up on the grip.

- Anchor your feet well into the sand.

- As in baseball, hinge your left arm at the elbow — no straight left arm here.

- Practice the swing once or twice.

- Swing slowly . . . try to punch the ball out to second base, not swing for the fences.

Ball inside bunker, feet outside. Again, the depth of the bunker determines how difficult this shot may be. Usually, the ball will be several inches below the level of your feet.

- Widen your stance.

- Play the ball back in your stance.

- Use only your lower body to get down to the ball — flex your knees, and don't bend at the waist.

- Try to hold the flex level throughout the swing.

- Hit the ball first, then the sand.

Plugged or buried lie. The secret to this shot is to dislodge as much sand as possible from just behind the ball. Counterintuitively, you want to close down the face of the club and make a sharp, steep swing without any attempt to follow through. The ball will usually pop out with topspin and run, so be careful if there are hazards across the green.

- Play the ball back in your stance.

- Grip the club a bit firmer.

- Make a steep backswing and hatchet the club into the sand just behind the ball.

- Abbreviate the follow-through . . . and try to leave the face buried in the sand.

- Hit it hard!

Downhill explosion. When you land on the downhill slope of a greenside bunker, escaping can be harder. The downward path of the swing will tend to deloft the clubface, and if you have to clear a high lip, that can be tricky. The secret? Align your shoulders to the slope.

- Widen your stance, and flex your knees more.

- Play the ball forward off your front foot.

- Make sure you swing down along the slope.

- Finish high. Get all the way through.

For pros like Tiger Woods, who practice sand shots by the hour, an explosion shot is simple.

Club caddie J. P. Wynne says that wet grips lead to bad swings. "The problem I see with bad weather and rain is that, no matter what, the player's grips always get wet. Once this happens, the player may hold the club tighter or in a different position because they do not feel comfortable. This then leads to erratic shots."

Another club caddie, Mike Danaher, suggests planning ahead for bad weather so one isn't caught out on the course unaware. "Extra clothes, an umbrella, dry towels, rain gear — these are only helpful if you have them with you when the weather turns," he says. "Look at the forecast and then picture yourself in that situation. It may not seem like 50 degrees is cold when you're in your house before the round, but after a few hours, it'll take more than a sweater and gloves to warm you up. If you bring them, and don't use them, no big deal. But if you don't bring them, it's hard to go back."

Making allowances for bad weather is the advice from club caddie Mike Maher. "Understanding that colder temperatures, wind, and rain will have an effect on your golf ball will allow you to address issues before they become a problem," he says. "For example, if it has been raining all day, you should realize that your 4-iron will not run up to the green like it usually does. Take the 3-iron."

Van Costa, longtime Tour caddie, calls bad weather "controlled mayhem" from the caddie's point of view. With all the extra towels and umbrellas, it can be difficult for a caddie to keep up, he admits. But his one bad-weather thought? "Keep the goddamn grips dry!" he says.

CHAPTER FOUR

Short and Sweet: Saving Strokes from 100 Yards and In

UP AND DOWN

We've already discussed the importance of the short game to your overall score. Shots from 100 yards can account for some 60 percent of your final score. Don't believe it? Let's say you are a scratch golfer and you go out and play a round of golf in even par: 36-36 for a 72. Nice round!

Now, assuming you've hit every fairway and green in regulation (and when was the last time someone even as good as Rory McIlroy did *that*? Answer: never), you made 14 shots from the tee with your driver. On those 14 holes, you made ten approach shots to the green with an iron, and on the four par-5 holes, you made four full-swing second shots with either a fairway wood or an iron. On the four par-3 holes, you hit each green with an iron or a wood. That's 32 full-swing shots.

Now, you made four approach shots from around 100 yards on the par 5s, and you two-putted every green. That's 40 shots from 100 yards and in, or 55 percent of your total score. Of course, if we analyzed your regular round's score, the number of full-swing shots would remain roughly the same, while the number of short-game shots — bunker shots, chip shots from off the green when you just missed an approach, pitches from in front of the green when you had to come out from under the trees, and, of course, three-putt greens — would rapidly increase. Track your individual statistics for a couple of rounds and see for yourself.

And yet, whenever we go to the practice range, we spend most of our time hitting full-swing shots, and very little practicing chipping, pitching, and lag putting. Does that make any sense?

It is in the short game that good and great rounds are made. If you could chip and pitch well, and keep the number of missed putts to a minimum, your score and your handicap would drop like a brand-new Titleist in a water hazard. And, in one of golf's

Opposite page: The old golf adage is correct: even the pros drive for show, but when it comes to putting, it's all about the Benjamins.

When it comes to the putting green, all that matters is getting the ball into the hole. Camilo Villegas does his Spiderman routine.

many frustrating little ironies, it is these short and simple shots, which require very little in terms of strength or sophisticated technique, that give most of us the most trouble.

Why is that? The lack of applied practice time is one good reason. Another is that the short game is where the pressure mounts in a round of golf. Usually, you are chipping or pitching or hitting a bunker shot because you've missed your previous shot, so you are upset and feel under pressure to get the ball close to the hole and recover (or at least discount) the results of that miss. And it is on the green, as that hoary bromide goes, where we "putt for dough" as opposed to the tee box's "drive for show." Smashing a driver off the tee is fun, and even if you go slightly awry there's a good chance you can continue to advance the ball with your next shot to the green. But a missed putt is a gut-twister, and that little tap-in you left on the edge of the hole counts exactly the same in your score as that massive tee ball.

Ironic? Put even an average golfer 100 yards from the green with a pitching wedge, and probably seven times out of ten they'll manage to hit the green. Most of us have a high degree of confidence with that club and that distance; there's nothing remotely scary about it. We've all made the shot a million times without trouble, and we therefore respond with a nice aggressive swing at the target, which results in a pretty good shot.

Now put that same golfer ten yards from the hole, tell them the goal is to get the ball within three feet (supposedly the easily made distance of a putt), and watch what happens. The shot takes less than a full swing, and one can use virtually any club in the bag, including the putter, and almost no strength at all. Yet the success rate for this kind of shot is perhaps three out of ten.

Dr. Sian Beilock, an expert on brain science and performance from the University of Chicago, has studied golfers, among others, for her book *Choke: What the Secrets of the Brain Reveal About*

Getting It Right When You Have To. She looks at why we often fail to perform certain tasks that are well within our capabilities, especially when the pressure is on. She cites *Blink* author Malcolm Gladwell's definition of "choking" as what happens when people lose their instinct and think too much about what they are doing. It's also called "paralysis by analysis," and almost every golfer can easily recall instances when this has happened. Indeed, because golf is a game that only proceeds when the player is ready, it is a fertile ground for the kind of mental gyrations that lead to choking.

Consider the three-foot putt. Anyone from an eight-year-old to an 80-year-old has the physical capabilities to make this shot. You can make a three-footer with your eyes closed, putting with one hand, backhanded, using the edge of a pitching wedge, or even the side of your foot (which, of course, is not allowed within the Rules of Golf). In other words, it is not a difficult shot in golf.

But when you *have* to make that three-footer to win the Masters, or even to beat Fred in your weekly two-dollar Nassau, the three-footer suddenly becomes the most problematic shot in the game. The only thing that has been added is the pressure of expectation. Self-doubt creeps in, the hands begin to shake, the mouth goes dry, the brain ceases to function, and the ball never touches the hole. Choke!

Dr. Beilock's recommendations for golfers include practicing stressful situations to get used to the feelings they awaken in our bodies (e.g., on the practice green, telling yourself, "This putt is to win the U.S. Open!"), and using deflectional techniques, such as counting backwards in threes or singing a song to yourself (silently, of course). This is way of releasing the hodgepodge of confusing thoughts that tend to creep in while standing over that three-footer, and letting brain and body do what is normally a pretty automatic activity: draining that putt.

What an inspiration! Paralyzed from the waist down. PCA adviser Dennis Walters (left) plays the Old Course at St. Andrews.

In this book, we've emphasized the importance of selecting a target for each and every shot. This is just as important for short-game shots as it is for full-swing shots, if not more so. Indeed, selecting the proper target on chips, pitches, and even putts goes a long way to making a successful shot. *The target is NOT the hole.* Let's say you've got a soft lob shot over a greenside bunker. Obviously, you want to get the ball to stop somewhere close to the hole (or, better yet, to go in). But the target should be a specific spot where you want the ball to *land* before it begins running toward the hole. That adds precision to the plan for the shot, and makes it easier to accomplish. Trying to hole a shot like this is a fool's errand. But picking out a spot on the green and figuring out how to hit the ball to land on that spot is a much simpler task than "getting it close." Of course, you select a spot based on how you envision the ball running after it lands, figuring in the break and speed of the green. And you may or may not be right. But playing to your target makes for a much easier, less stressful situation, and your swing will likely be smoother and more confident.

Play a round of golf where you try to hit your targets, not the hole. Grade yourself on how close you can get to hitting the target you select, especially on those little chips and pitches around the green. You will likely find this a bit difficult at first, because we are all trained to be hole-centric; the hole is, after all, the ultimate destination. But if you can marshal the mental discipline to think about each shot as moving the ball from Point

A (where it now rests) to Point B (the spot on the green where you want the ball to land) you'll begin to see unusual results: the ball ends up near Point C (the hole).

In the short game, there is an almost infinite variety in how you get the ball to the hole. For a 40-foot shot from the greenside fringe, you can select a lofted club and plan to land it halfway to the hole, letting it run the last 20 feet. Or you can select a less-lofted club, such as an 8- or 9-iron, and plan to have it fly ten feet, then run the last 30 feet. The lie of the ball, the slope of the green, and the conditions of the day are all contributing factors in deciding how to play such a shot. But there should always be a target, and that target should be kept in the forefront of your mind when making the shot. And the shot you select should be a green light; you should have the utmost confidence that you can make the shot.

Let it be said that caddies almost universally recommend getting a chip shot on the ground as soon as possible, and they strongly encourage a chip-and-run, or even a putt from off the green, over a lofted flop shot. That's because most caddies know that the success rate for the lofted pitch is much lower, especially for average golfers and those not named Phil Mickelson.

PUTTING

Stroking a golf ball to roll across the well tended grass of a green so that it falls into the hole is another one of those deceptively easy-to-do activities that's hard to do consistently well. Physically, putting requires almost no effort. Mentally? Entire books have been written about how to overcome the mind-born phantoms that make you see a break that isn't there, or fail to see one that is. And then there is "the yips," that strange paranormal state where just the simple act of dragging the putterhead backwards a few inches — never mind a smooth through-stroke — becomes nearly impossible.

Davis Love (in blue shirt) and caddie John Burke (behind him) use teamwork on the putting green.

91

Even the prep work that player and caddie perform before making a putt is relatively easy. There are two basic conditions to consider: line and speed. The line is just that: the imaginary line you see running between the ball and the hole, adjusted to compensate for the tilt of the green from side to side and uphill and downhill. The speed of the putt, or how hard you strike the ball, is determined by the distance you are from the hole, plus the allowance made for the ball rolling either uphill or down.

But because those two calculations must be correctly gauged and then applied by the player in the stroke, and because the rolling ball may be deflected ever so slightly by a spike mark, a footprint depression, a gust of wind, a bug, a piece of sand, or almost anything else, the outcome of the putt is always in doubt. And that's the sport of it. You guess, you try, and you see what happens.

Golfers with a caddie will benefit by having a second pair of eyes to look at each putt and either confirm or question the player's conclusions about the putt. The caddie will usually take the "macro" approach to a putt, that is, determine the overarching conditions that will affect a putt. They are usually threefold:

1. The orientation of the course to the local terrain. Every golf course lies on a piece of the Earth that will slope toward or away from the local low and high points. In the Coachella Valley of Palm Springs, everything slopes toward Indio, the city at the lowest point. Near the ocean, most courses will tend to slope toward the water. In the mountains, courses will slope away from the highest peak. Elsewhere, there is usually a tilt, pronounced or subtle, in one direction or another. You can figure out the orientation of the course you play, most often with just a moment's thought.

2. The orientation of the green to the course. As we've said before, golf course architects can be tricky dudes. Sometimes, they'll put in greens that slope away from the line of approach, and sometimes they'll build them against the general orientation of the course itself. But most of the time, greens will follow the overall characteristics of the terrain.

One of the keys to determining the orientation of the green is to find its low and high points. Generally speaking, that's the orientation of that green, and that's the way the ball will tend to break. As former Tour caddie and now architecture editor of *Golfweek* Brad Klein recommends, "Ask yourself: 'If I were water, which way would I go?'"

3. The orientation of the putt. This is the last piece of the puzzle. First consider the larger forces at work in the putt by recalling or reminding yourself of the first two, and then begin to zero in on the curvatures between your ball and the hole. Knowing the orientation of the course in general, and this green in particular, will be helpful in determining how much, or how little, your putt will be affected by the slopes between the ball and the hole.

With this wide-to-narrow focus, a caddie will be able to determine with some precision which way the ball will break and by how much. Then the player and the caddie can focus on all the local elements of the putt that will come into play: grain, uphill or downhill slope, weather conditions, and wind. Once those are factored in, it should be pretty easy to determine a useful line for the putt.

Most amateur players *underestimate* the amount of break they think they see. Which is why most of us tend to miss our putts "on the low side," or on the downhill side of a curving putt. Tour caddies who watch a lot of amateurs in the weekly pro-am warm-up events see this week in and week out. As an experiment, during your next practice round, resolve to add at least two inches of break to every putt you attempt (three-footers and less excepted). You will be amazed at the results.

Straight Lines and Curves

Are You a Right-Brain or a Left-Brain Putter?

Golf guru Mike Shannon, who works out of the Sea Island Golf Learning Center in Georgia, has done a lot of work with putters, whom he puts into one of two categories: linear and nonlinear.

Linear putters are left-brain dominant: they are logical, sequential, and tend to make lists and do things in an orderly manner. In putting, they tend to see things in straight lines: if they read a putt as breaking six inches, they "see" the correct line of the putt as a straight line between the ball and that point six inches to the side of the hole. They then just try to hit the putt the correct speed along the line.

Nonlinear putters are influenced by the right hemisphere of the brain. They are emotional, intuitive, and tend to do whatever feels right at that moment, rather than in a left-brained, orderly manner. And on the green, they don't "see" straight lines; they see the putts as curved lines breaking into the hole.

Knowing which kind of putter you are is invaluable in aiming. Linear putters should make sure they can see that perfect straight line before taking the club back. Even more importantly, they should use the alignment aids on the golf ball and the putterhead itself to make sure the initial direction of the strike is on the straight line they've determined. Once that line is decided, they can then forget it and concentrate on the speed.

Nonlinear putters probably shouldn't waste a lot of time making sure the little guideline or the logo of the ball is set to a particular line. Doing that might even be counterproductive. Instead, turn the ball so that nothing but white dimples shows when you're standing over the putt. For aiming, pretend the hole is a clock face, with six o'clock on the edge facing the ball, and determine where on the clock the ball should fall into the hole. For left-to-right breaks, it will be anywhere from nine to six. For right to left, from three to six. Straight putts are either dead-on six, or just to one side or the other. By envisioning the ball curving and falling into the cup at the right point, you are reinforcing your natural tendency to see curved lines, and your putts will improve.

Having an experienced caddie like Ronan Flood provide a second read on the greens has helped Padraig Harrington win three major tournaments.

TOUCH AND FEEL

Of the two main elements in putting, line and speed, most amateurs would improve their games more by concentrating on speed. Getting the ball to the hole is not just the only way it's ever going to drop in, but being able to correctly judge the speed of each putt will help eliminate that dreaded bane of low scores: the three-putt. Trying to make those four-footers you've left short or overcooked will add gray to anyone's hair and increase the amount of stomach acid.

To be able to stroke the ball so that it finishes within 18 inches of the hole requires that kind of subjective talent known as "touch" or "feel." There's no way to teach feel in putting; you've either got it or you don't. And it can come and go. But a good putting touch comes to those who pay attention to the "micro" conditions of the putting surface. It helps to be able to recognize the grain of the grass and determine which way it is growing. (See sidebar, Straight Lines and Curves, p. 94.)

It always helps to spend at least 15 minutes before a round warming up on the practice putting green. At most golf courses, you'll get a pretty good indication of how fast the greens are running that day. But greens vary from hole to hole and even from the practice green to real ones, so you can't depend on the feedback you get from the practice putting you do . . . just get the first indication of the speed.

Out on the course, where the putts matter, there are other things you can do to get a feel for the speed of the

Watching another player's putt is one of the ways Phil Mickelson and caddie Bones Mackay pick up knowledge on the green.

greens on the course you're playing:

Watch the ball after it lands on the green. Did your approach shot hit and stick? Or did it run a few yards once it landed? You can deduce whether the greens are hard or soft, running fast or slow, by watching the ball once it lands.

Watch your playing partners' putts. If the others in your group putt before you do, pay close attention to their putts and how they roll out. Watch to see how hard the player hits the putt, and watch to see how it reacts as it nears the hole. Obviously, if another player is putting on roughly your same line, only from further away, it's a great idea to study her putt to see how the ball does on both line and speed. But even if she's putting on a totally different line, you can learn a great deal by watching her speed control.

Walk the line. If it doesn't delay play, walk alongside the line you plan to hit your putt (don't walk *in* the actual line, as your footprints can create depressions in the grass that could throw the ball offline). Many golfers can get valuable feedback from their feet on the green's slopes and grades. Use that feedback to reinforce or double-check what your eyes tell you.

NURTURING FEEL

When you've got good feel on the putting green, everyone knows it. Your putts begin to drop, or just lip out. As a result, your confidence soars, your stroke is loose and free, and you feel like the hole is as big as a washtub.

Then there are the days when you've got about as much feel as a cement block. You leave one putt five feet short, then on the next green, hit one that goes ten feet past. Your stroke seems off, it speeds up, you grasp the putter tighter and tighter, and you begin to compute just how many dollars you're going to lose today. Not fun.

What's the difference? When you're putting with confidence and feel, you usually aren't thinking about anything except making the putt. You don't think about the size of your backswing, where your hands are, how hard to hit the putt . . . you just see and react. It's like being on automatic pilot.

When you're putting badly, you're subject to that "paralysis by analysis" problem. Which means your head is full of all kinds of extraneous things. You wonder why your left pinky finger is aching. You see the putter moving back and it looks like it's moving in a circular direction, so you have to adjust midswing. You don't see lines anywhere, and you just hope you can keep the ball on the green.

Were it possible, putting with a completely empty head (think a flatline EEG!) would be optimal. Your brain could then make the line-speed calculation without any interference, and making a putt would be as easy as catching a fly ball. That is why Dr. Sian Beilock recommends counting backwards by threes or singing a song to oneself when trying to make an important putt. Either of those devices will in effect empty your head of extraneous thoughts and let your inner golf brain take over unimpeded.

There are other methods for freeing your mind on the putting green. You can try them out on the practice green or even try them on the course:

Close your eyes. The best way to get your feel back is to feel it. Try this: line up your putt and go through your usual pre-putt routine. Then, just before you pull the club back, close your eyes and keep them closed while you strike the ball. If you can, keep them closed until you hear the putt rattle into the cup (or your partner says, "Darn!"). By eliminating your visual picture, your brain and body will take over and make the putter swing automatically, without any last-second influence from you. If you've read the putt correctly and kept the target in your mind's eye, you'll find most of your eyes-closed putts will either go in or just miss. Once you've done this a few times, you should begin to regain that confident sense.

Look at the hole. If keeping your eyes closed is a little too drastic for you, you can get the same effect by striking the putt while your eyes are looking at the hole (or the target, as the case may be). Again, this helps ensure you won't be "ball-bound" while standing over a putt, and encourages a free-flowing, natural swing in response to the target.

Change your grip. The Rules of Golf permit you to hold your putter any way you want (as long as you grip it on the handle or shaft and strike the ball with the head). When all else fails, it can sometimes help to fix a balky putter by changing the way you grip it. Try left-hand low. Or modify your right-hand-low grip by putting your forefinger down the grip or some other way. Try "the Claw." Putt left-handed. The point of the exercise is to introduce something that feels odd, unusual, or slightly uncomfortable to your putting stroke. By doing this, you will actually begin to think only of moving the clubface backwards and forwards in this strange new way, and instantly forget all the other analytic nonsense that is keeping you from making the best stroke.

Joe Pyland, longtime caddie for Boo Weekley, advises amateur golfers to focus on speed over line. "Try and change your mindset about medium-to-long approach putts," Pyland says, "especially the moderately straight ones. All the amateurs I see standing over these putts are thinking about speed in a totally defensive way. They are really just lagging, kind of randomly, toward a semicircle that is left, short, and right of the hole. Instead, start with the line, commit to the line, and pick a speed that truly gives the putt a chance to go in. If it goes by five feet and everybody groans, don't listen to them, 'cause they're all just scared laggers themselves."

Nick Watney's caddie, Tim Goodell, relates how players and caddies scout the hole locations for the tournament during practice and think about where the short-game shots may come from. "Amateur golfers who watch a PGA Tour practice round will notice that caddies and players do a lot of extra practicing when they get to a green," he says. "That's based on the four days of pin positions and all the different areas of the green where we will have putts and chips of different angles. During the practice round, we will rehearse various scenarios for getting up and down based on the four cup positions."

Eric Miller, caddie for Jerry Kelly, concurs. "The amateur golfer should look around for the real no-go side of the green and concentrate his extra chip and bunker shots and putts away from that area," Miller says. "In the competitive rounds, you should be playing to the safe sides, and you'll want to feel like you've tried, or at least considered, a lot of shots in those areas."

From the first tee to the last putt, you should approach every shot like a caddie does: as a problem that must be solved. Solving that individual problem begins with the correct assessment of the conditions (using the Five-Finger Format), making a calm assessment of the best shot to reach the target (the green-light special), and finally, making an aggressive swing at the target you've selected. This way of playing the game works just as well on a two-foot putt as it does on a 300-yard drive. And it will help most players avoid making difficult situations worse, going from trouble to disaster.

Tour Championship winner Bill Haas and his brother and caddie, Jay Hass Jr., go over their strategy for a hole at the 2011 PGA Championship.

Bunkered

Bob Tway's Remarkable Shot Won the 1986 PGA in Dramatic Fashion

Australian Greg Norman is probably fated to be long remembered in golf history not for all his many wins (including two British Open titles), but for all the majors he lost on the last day. In 1986, for instance, Norman was the tournament leader going into the final round at all four major championships. He only managed to win the British Open at Turnberry.

His reputation as Fate's Favorite Punching Bag, however, probably began a few weeks after that victory, when the PGA Championship was staged at Toledo's historic Inverness Club. After Saturday's third round, Norman led the field by four shots over Bob Tway, who had shot into contention with a third-round 64. The two were paired for the final round, which was postponed to Monday due to severe weather.

Moving to the back nine of the final round, Norman's four-shot lead began to waver. On the par-4 11th hole, Norman made a double-bogey 6 to Tway's routine 4. The lead was cut in half. On the par-5 13th, Tway nailed a 1-iron on the green with his second shot and two-putted for a birdie. Now he trailed by just one. And when a poor drive led to a bogey for Norman on the next hole, they were tied.

Tway's caddie that day was Mark Jimenez, and he remembers the duel down the stretch. Both men parred 15, 16, and 17. Tway managed a par on the penultimate hole despite a difficult lie in the rough next to the 17th green. "On the 17th, he hit it right of the green and into just an awful lie in the rough," Jimenez recalls. "Bob asked the official if someone had stepped on his ball while looking for it in the rough, but he said no. It was down, buried, almost unhittable." Instead, Tway managed to flop his ball out onto the green, where it finished some three feet from the hole, and he made the knee-knocker to stay tied.

Norman split the fairway with his drive on 18, while Tway's shot drifted into more rough down the right. From another troublesome lie, he was only able to get his approach shot into the front-left bunker at the green. Norman hit the green with his approach, but his ball spun back onto the front fringe, some 20 feet from the hole.

Tway looked at his bunker shot, heart sinking. The ball had just dribbled into the bunker and come to rest on a downhill slope. Making matters worse, the green sloped away from him and Inverness's greens were running icy fast.

According to Jimenez, Tway opened up the face of his sand wedge (to counteract the downhill slope, which tends to shut down the clubface) and made an aggressive swing. The ball popped out, landing about a foot on the green, and began to roll. And roll. And roll. Into the cup. Tway began leaping around in the bunker like a maddened stork, and the crowd went wild.

Norman, of course, still had a chance to tie, but going hard to make his long putt, he ran it past the hole about ten feet, and then missed the comebacker. He lost the title by two shots, one of which remains among the most miraculous in golf's long and storied history.

Inverness caddie master Tom Grzywinski was standing near the last green, in part to watch the action and in part to fulfill his duty by collecting caddie bibs as the men came off the course. "When the ball went in, I was like 'Oh my God . . . did you see that?'" he recalled years later. But he kept his wits about him enough to get Tway's winning golf ball from Jimenez, and it remains today proudly on display in the Inverness clubhouse.

Some months after Tway's miraculous shot, the editors of a golf magazine arranged to bring him back to Inverness to step into that same bunker, to try to make the shot again. He took about 20 swings that day, made none, and only had a couple of balls finish close. "The one shot that felt the most like the one at the PGA slid past the hole a good six feet," he said. "I'd have hated to have to make that one for the championship!"

And Norman? He came back to Inverness in 1993 when the PGA Championship was again awarded to the club. And again, he came to the last hole with a chance to win the tournament with a birdie putt. This time, the ball disappeared into the hole, only to pop back out and stop on the lip. That meant a playoff for the title with Paul Azinger, who eventually won on the second playoff hole when Norman three-putted.

Azinger's caddie that day? None other than Mark Jimenez. Who says the golfing gods don't have a sense of humor?

Longtime pro Bob Tway was the first to stick a dagger into Greg Norman, holing out a bunker shot on the last hole of the 1986 PGA Championship.

Rules to Live By: Knowing Your Options Can Save You Strokes

One of the fundamental principles underlying the Rules of Golf is that "you put your ball in play at the start of the hole, play only your own ball, and do not touch it until you lift it from the hole." Alas, the game is not always so simple. As we observed elsewhere in this book, "Trouble is a major part of the game of golf." When our shots stray from the fairways and greens, and our balls become lost or end up in forbidding areas like bunkers and water hazards, the Rules of Golf impose penalties and, more important, provide us with certain options for how to proceed.

Every game has rules. Some games, and rules, are simpler than others. In tennis, for example, you can learn the basic rules in one session: hit the ball over the net and keep it between the lines. Pretty simple. (At least, in concept.)

Golf, on the other hand, is governed by a fairly complex body of rules that has evolved over centuries, starting in the mid-18th century when a group of golfers in Scotland first wrote down what they understood to be the rules of the ancient game. The rules continue to evolve under the auspices of the two ruling bodies of golf: the United States Golf Association (USGA) and the Royal and Ancient Golf Club of St. Andrews, Scotland (known simply as R&A). There are 34 rules, supplemented by a rather thick book of rules decisions issued by the USGA and R&A as new situations arise.

Just like developing your "inner caddie" can help you make the right decisions about what type of shots to play in difficult situations, developing your "inner rules official" is essential to selecting the right options and minimizing the damage to your score when your errant shots take you to the inhospitable nooks and crannies of the course. "Rules management," like "course management," is an essential part of the game.

Surprisingly, many casual golfers never take the time to

Opposite page: Experienced caddies like PCA Caddie Hall of Famer Mike "Fluff" Cowan (left), who works for Jim Furyk, understand that the Rules of Golf can often be utilized to save a stroke or two.

acquaint themselves with even some of the most basic rules of the game. This chapter does not attempt to provide an overview of all of the rules. There are a number of books on the market that do that. Rather, after explaining *why* the self-enforcement of the rules is fundamental to the "spirit of the game," this chapter reviews the rules that govern various problem situations and explains *how* they may be used to your advantage.

THE SPIRIT OF THE GAME

The game of golf is unique in its reliance on players to observe the "spirit of the game" by adhering to the rules and imposing penalties on themselves even when no other competitor (or an official) is aware of a violation. In most competitive sports, officials are charged with detecting violations of the rules and imposing penalties or calling infractions. Of course, referees in sports such as football and basketball cannot see everything that occurs on the field or court, and inevitably some violations go undetected. How many times have you watched a football game and heard a commentator remark, "That was a clear hold. Jones got away with one there"?

In most sports, a violation that escapes the eye of an official is simply one of the breaks of the game. Players are taught to push the rules to the limit. Anything goes, as long as you don't get caught. Can you imagine an offensive lineman walking up to a referee after a play and saying, "Excuse me, sir. I held number 74 on that play, and my team should be assessed a 10-yard penalty"? Or a tennis player at Wimbledon insisting that his shot was out when the line judge called it in? These no doubt would be career-limiting moves.

In golf, on the other hand, players (if they take the game seriously) must police themselves. Most golf competitions are conducted without rules officials watching over every shot.

Even at professional and top-tier amateur events, rarely is there a sufficient number of officials to supervise all of the play. The introduction to the Rules of Golf explains the "spirit of the game" as follows:

> Golf is played, for the most part, without the supervision of a referee or umpire. The game relies on the integrity of the individual to show consideration for other players and to abide by the Rules. All players should conduct themselves in a disciplined manner, demonstrating courtesy and sportsmanship at all times, irrespective of how competitive they may be. This is the spirit of the game of golf.

Examples abound of golfers adhering to the spirit of the game by calling penalties on themselves — often at enormous cost. In 2005, Adam Van Houten, a high school sophomore, shot a two-round total of 144 to win the Ohio Division II golf tournament by six strokes. However, after signing his scorecard, he realized he had recorded a score for one hole that was one stroke less than he had actually scored. Although the stroke in question had no bearing on the outcome of the tournament, Van Houten nevertheless reported the error, knowing that having signed an incorrect scorecard, he would be disqualified. His integrity and dedication to the spirit of the game cost him the state title. However, he later received one of *Sports Illustrated* magazine's "Sportsmanship of the Decade" awards.

Adhering to the spirit of the game can also have sizable financial consequences. In a sudden-death playoff at the Verizon Heritage tournament in 2010, Brian Davis pulled his approach shot on the 18th hole of Harbour Town Golf Links into a hazard. Since his opponent, Jim Furyk, had hit the green, Davis elected to play a difficult shot from the beach, which was strewn with grasses and debris, rather than taking a penalty stroke and dropping out of the hazard. He played a good shot, leaving himself with a lengthy putt for par.

However, on his backswing, Davis's clubhead almost imperceptibly grazed a loose reed in the hazard. He notified an official, and, after some discussion and a review of videotape, he was penalized two strokes under Rule 13-4c, which prohibits touching a "loose impediment" in a hazard (other than during the "stroke," which is defined as the forward movement of the club and does not include the backswing). As a result, Davis lost his opportunity to save par and continue the playoff after Furyk parred the hole. The difference between first and second place (not to mention the intangible benefits of winning his first PGA Tour event): roughly $400,000.

Davis received over 100 messages praising his integrity. Furyk commented that it was "not the way I wanted to win. It's obviously a tough loss for him, and I respect and admire what he did." Davis, who told Furyk that he could not have lived with himself had he not reported the violation, later stated, "I am proud to uphold the values that my parents taught me, and I teach my kids the same stuff. Be honest in your sport and in your life and simply do your best. That's all you can do." Tournament Director Slugger White summed it up best: "This will come back to him in spades, tenfold."

Another reason that self-enforcement of the rules is integral to the game of golf is that, unlike most other sports where players are in direct, physical competition, the golfer essentially plays against the course itself. "Old Man Par" is a formidable opponent. Only by the adherence to a uniform set of rules can one round of golf fairly be compared to another. (The scores of many weekend golfers no doubt would be significantly higher if they adhered strictly to the rules; it's a bit like comparing apples to oranges.)

Moreover, the integrity of the handicap system, which permits golfers of different levels of ability to compete, depends upon an adherence to a uniform set of rules.

HISTORY AND DEVELOPMENT OF THE RULES

The first recorded rules of golf were issued in 1744 by the Honourable Company of Gentlemen Golfers in Edinburgh, Scotland, and consisted of 13 "Articles & Laws in Playing at Golf." Some of the rules reflect the quite different nature of the game played over the inhospitable links of 18th-century Scotland. Except on the "fair Green," stones, bones, or broken clubs could not be removed in playing a shot. (The modern rules are more liberal. See Rule 23: "Loose Impediments.") Article 10 provided: "If a Ball be stopp'd by any Person, Horse, Dog, or anything else, The Ball so stop'd must be play'd where it lyes." (This is the precursor of Rule 19-1; horses, dogs, and spectators are now termed "outside agencies.")

Today, the codification and amendment of the Rules of Golf are the responsibility of the USGA and the R&A. There are 34 rules, beginning with Rule 1-1, which states succinctly: "The Game of Golf consists of playing a ball with a club from the teeing ground into the hole by a stroke or successive strokes in accordance with the Rules." The rules are prefaced by a set of definitions, which are essential to anyone understanding them. (However, you won't find "mulligan" or "gimmie" among them.)

Of course, no matter how specific the rules might be, we all know that any set of rules or laws is invariably subject to interpretation when concrete (sometimes unanticipated) situations are confronted. Accordingly, the rules are supplemented by a volume of rules decisions issued by the USGA and the R&A. The decisions explain the application of the rules to actual situations that arise in competition. The decisions have the same binding force as the rules themselves.

While at times the Rules of Golf present complexities, one of the fundamental principles underlying the rules is that you "play the course as you find it." The player must accept the conditions he or she encounters during play. This principle is embodied in Rule 13-1, which states that "the ball must be played as it lies, except as otherwise provided in the Rules." It might seem unfair to have to play a shot out of a divot or other poor lie in the fairway, but the 18th-century Scotsmen who developed the first rules did not seem preoccupied with fairness.

USING THE RULES TO YOUR ADVANTAGE IN DIFFICULT SITUATIONS

Just like your "inner caddie" can help you make the right decisions about what type of shot to hit in difficult situations, tapping your "inner rules official" can help you identify your options when you encounter problems. Unless you know all your options, you won't be in a position to evaluate the best option to extricate yourself from the situation you face or to minimize the damage. As someone once said, "Knowledge is power," and every golfer can learn to use rules knowledge to his or her advantage in a variety of situations.

Bunkers

First, a bit of terminology. Contrary to popular belief, the term "sand trap" does not appear anywhere in the Rules of Golf or the golf lexicon. If your ball is in a hollowed-out area filled with sand, it's in a bunker. Since a bunker is a hazard, there are certain things you can't do when your ball is in a bunker. For example, you are not allowed to ground your club before making a stroke, or to move loose impediments. Thus, a critical threshold question is whether, in fact, your ball is in a bunker. As Dustin

Johnson learned to his chagrin at the 2010 PGA Championship at Whistling Straits, this issue is not always so clear-cut. (See sidebar, When Is a Bunker Not a Bunker?, p. 112.)

The rules define a bunker as "a prepared area of ground, often a hollow, from which turf or soil has been removed and replaced with sand or the like." Note, however, that the grass-covered ground bordering or within a bunker is not part of the bunker. This includes a turf face of a bunker. So, if your ball is lying in such an area, the hazard restrictions don't apply. In addition, sand that has spilled outside the margin of the bunker is not considered part of the bunker.

On most well-manicured courses, a golfer will rarely confront the bunker boundary question. However, some courses contain expansive "waste areas" on the peripheries of holes that contain sand and resemble bunkers, but are not treated as hazards under local rules. Oftentimes, golf carts might even traverse such areas. If your ball is in such an area, you may ground your club and remove loose impediments. Always be familiar with local rules.

Whether you are entitled to relief from a plugged ball may depend on whether you are in a bunker. If your ball is embedded in the sand in the lip of a bunker, you're out of luck. (You might consider the unplayable ball option, discussed below.) But if the ball is plugged in the turf face of the bunker, and the course has adopted a local rule permitting relief anywhere "through the green" (any area of the course other than the teeing ground or the putting green of the hole you're

Tiger Woods demonstrates his "world-class finish" at the end of a bunker shot.

When Is a Bunker Not a Bunker?

Dustin Johnson's Calamity at Whistling Straits

Local rules often determine whether certain bunker-like features of courses are treated as hazards. Unfortunately, Dustin Johnson didn't take the time to familiarize himself with the local rules at the 2010 PGA Championship at Whistling Straits.

Standing on the 18th tee on Sunday, Johnson led the tournament by a stroke. He had birdied two of the last three holes of Pete Dye's somewhat bizarre, brutal, links-like course to put himself in position to win his first major championship.

Tragically, the long-hitting Johnson lost his tee shot wide right, and the ball sailed outside the gallery ropes into a forbidding area dominated by irregular mounds, bunkers, and tall fescue grass. When Johnson arrived at his ball, it was resting on sand, which was strewn in some areas with grass and was hard packed, as a consequence of hundreds of spectators who had strolled through the area during the course of the tournament.

Johnson sized up his shot. He played a 4-iron toward the green of the difficult 18th hole, which had yielded only one birdie that day. He ultimately missed a seven-foot putt for par that would have won the tournament, and headed toward the 10th tee to join Martin Kaymer and Bubba Watson for a three-person playoff.

Not so fast. A rules official pulled him aside and notified him of a problem: Johnson might have grounded his club in a bunker, in which case he would be assessed a two-stroke penalty. "What bunker?" responded the dumbfounded Johnson. That question would prove to be a matter of controversy in the golf world for the following week, and no doubt for years to come. Rather than participating in the playoff, Johnson finished tied for fifth.

Johnson claimed that he reasonably assumed that his ball was resting on a grassy area that had been stomped down by foot traffic. "It never crossed my mind that I was in a bunker," he says. He was. Perhaps only at Whistling Straits would such a controversy arise. Dye designed the course, which skirts the shore of Lake Michigan in northern Wisconsin, to mimic a links course. The course is carved out of a vast expanse of sandy, irregular, and severe terrain, and contains roughly ten times the number of bunkers typically found on a course. In fact, no one, not even the superintendent, knows precisely how many bunkers litter Whistling Straits; they tend to blend into the rugged landscape.

Bunkers that are worn down by pedestrian and vehicular traffic, or the margins of which are obscured by throngs of spectators, might more appropriately be treated as waste areas. (Children were even spotted building sand castles in some of the bunkers at Whistling Straits.) However, the PGA decided that all of the myriad of bunkers strewn across the vast, desolate outer fringes of Whistling Straits would be treated as hazards, rather than waste areas. The local rules sheet, as well as notices posted in the locker room, made that clear. Johnson conceded that he never read the local rules sheet.

The lesson: when you play on an unfamiliar course, take the time to learn the local rules. Rules ignorance might not cost you a major championship, but it could be the difference between winning or losing your $5 Nassau.

Dustin Johnson, who didn't realize he was in a bunker, grounded his club and lost the 2010 PGA Championship at Whistling Straits.

playing, or a hazard), you are entitled to lift, clean, and drop (or, in some cases, to place) your ball. Absent such a local rule, relief is allowed only in "closely mown areas," such as fairways, and the turf face of a bunker is not a closely mown area.

How many times have you played after extensive rain and confronted a ball in a bunker filled with water? Generally, you have to take your hazards as you find them. However, you are entitled to relief from casual water in a bunker. You may drop the ball at the closest spot in the bunker that provides relief and is not nearer the hole. If the entire bunker is covered by water, your relief is limited to finding a shallower spot. (You may also drop the ball outside of the bunker at the cost of a penalty stroke.)

Let's say you're playing on a links course and experience the misfortune of finding your ball nestled deeply in a sinister pot bunker (one of those small but deep, sand-filled pits most often found on links-style courses near the sea). Your sand game is no match for this foe. You could easily envision taking several futile strokes in the bunker without extricating your ball from its clutches. The unplayable ball rule (discussed below) gives you another option: declare the ball unplayable, take a penalty stroke, and play from the spot of your previous shot (taking extra care to avoid a return to the pot bunker). Know your limitations, and your options. Sometimes surrendering in a small skirmish can advance the overall campaign.

Water Hazards

Probably no areas of golf courses strike more fear into the hearts of weekend golfers than water hazards. Although we often lose balls in the woods or other inhospitable areas, there is something particularly deflating to the psyche to see your brand-new Titleist Pro V1 plunge into a watery abyss (especially when your playing partners needle you about the mishap). Unlike the pros, who tend to think more rationally, the mere sight of a water hazard can induce traumatic thoughts and stress that make it all but impossible for the casual golfer to maintain his or her normal pre-shot routine or to achieve a smooth stroke.

Ironically, the rules governing water hazards are actually less punitive, and afford more options, than the rules governing balls that are lost in other areas of the course or that land out of bounds. (In the latter situations, the "stroke-and-distance" penalty applies — you must return to the spot from where you played your last shot, with a one-stroke penalty.) So, while watching your ball plunge to unrecoverable depths might not be the highlight of your round, knowing the water hazard rules can substantially lessen the pain and minimize the damage to your score.

Keep in mind that the water hazard rules apply only if it is "known or virtually certain" that your ball was lost in a water hazard, and not in some other part of the course. So, if you hit your ball over a ridge out of sight in the general direction of a water hazard, and it's possible that it landed in the woods bordering the hazard, you must apply the lost-ball rule. A rules decision (26-1/1) explains this concept.

The water hazard rules distinguish between generic water hazards and "lateral water hazards," and knowing this distinction is critical to determining your options. In either case, a player taking relief from the hazard is assessed a one-stroke penalty. However, lateral hazards provide more relief options.

Of course, the player is always free to play the ball from the hazard, whether it is actually resting in water or on ground inside the margin of the hazard. It is tempting to undertake such heroic shots and avoid the one-stroke penalty. Oftentimes, however, considering the lie and your skill level, it is more prudent to take your medicine (the penalty stroke) and play a shot you are capable of executing (think green light), rather than ending up in a deeper part of the hazard.

Some years ago, Tiger Woods putted off of the 13th green of Augusta National during the Masters Tournament. He had a downhill putt from the back of the slick green, and the ball picked up speed, rolled down the slope at the front of the green, and came to rest in a shallow part of Rae's Creek. He was not a happy camper, but, rather than taking relief from the hazard, he proceeded to pitch the ball from the creek onto the green. But what works for Tiger might not work as well for the casual golfer. Most golfers would have been better served taking a penalty stroke and re-putting the ball (with a gentler stroke).

Keep in mind also that you may not ground your club before playing a shot from a hazard. Touching water or tall grass with your club is not grounding; to ground the club, you must rest it on grass to the point that the grass is compressed. There is no penalty for making a stroke at a ball that is moving in a water hazard, although this strategy is in most cases ill advised.

Generic water hazards, such as a pond in front of a green, are marked by yellow stakes or lines. If your ball is in such a hazard, you have two relief options:

1. Play from the spot from which you last played.

2. Drop a ball behind the water hazard on an imaginary line demarcated by the hole and the point at which the ball last crossed the margin of the hazard. There is no limit to how far behind the hazard you may drop the ball.

This rule requires a careful consideration of the options. In many cases, the second option will permit a shorter shot. However, the topography of some holes, such as a severely downhill par 3 with a pond fronting the green, might afford no workable drop area, and playing a second ball from the tee may be the best option. (Keep in mind that if you are playing from the back tees and there are other teeing grounds along your permitted drop ine, you may drop a ball on another teeing ground.)

Also, be aware that courses sometimes create drop zones (typically on par-3 holes requiring long carries over water) that provide an additional option. These are typically marked by white circles, and should be (but often are not) noted on the scorecard.

Now let's turn to "lateral water hazards," which are marked by red stakes or lines. The classic lateral hazard is a creek running along the periphery of a hole in a parallel fashion. If your ball lands in a lateral hazard, you have the same options you would have in the case of a generic water hazard. However, you also have two additional options, which reflect the fact that it is often not possible or practical to drop the ball "behind" a lateral hazard:

1. Drop a ball outside the hazard (but no closer to the hole), within two club-lengths of the point where the ball last crossed the margin of the hazard.

2. Drop a ball outside the hazard, within two club-lengths of a point on the opposite margin (the other side) of the hazard that is the same distance from the hole as the point where the ball last crossed the hazard. (As a practical matter, this option is seldom advantageous. A rules decision (26-1/15) contains a diagram outlining the lateral hazard options.)

How do you identify where the ball last crossed the margin of the hazard? Obviously, the player (sometimes consulting with his playing partners or opponents) must simply make an educated guess. Keep in mind, however, that a ball might cross the margin of a hazard more than once, and it is the last crossing that fixes the point of relief.

Once again, knowing the lateral water hazard rule is critical. Only if you know all your options can you determine your best option in any situation. The ability to drop a ball outside of the hazard within two club-lengths of the point where the ball last crossed the margin of the lateral hazard often will be more advantageous than playing from the spot where the ball was last played or dropping behind the hazard. Some bodies of water might be marked in part with yellow stakes and in part with red stakes, so that different rules apply, depending on where the ball last crossed the hazard margin.

When Is Your Ball Unplayable? Whenever You Want It to Be
The unplayable ball rule is probably one of the least understood rules among casual golfers. It is also a rule that can provide relief (at the price of a penalty stroke) from any number of difficult situations.

Consider the following situation. Mike and Jim are playing a match under match-play rules. Jim has putted out for a bogey on a par-4 hole. Mike has a birdie putt from three feet above the hole on a severely sloping double-tiered green. His putt slides by the cup, picks up speed, rolls onto the lower tier of the green, and then proceeds to roll off the green into a cavernous bunker. Assessing the shot, he'd be lucky to get out of the bunker, much less make a bogey. Jim figures he's won the hole. He's shocked by what happens next.

"I'm declaring my ball unplayable," says Mike. He lifts the ball from the bunker, places it at the spot from where he putted, holes the putt, and, with a one-stroke penalty, takes a bogey, halving the hole. Jim is incredulous. "You can't do that!" he says. "You have to play the ball from the bunker!" Who is correct?

Mike properly invoked the unplayable ball rule. The decision as to whether a ball is unplayable is completely within the discretion of the player. The ball does not have to be in a hole, next to a rock or tree root, or in some other spot where playing the shot is impossible or impracticable. In short, unplayability is in the eye of the beholder. (The one exception is if the ball lies in a water hazard. In that case, the player must apply the water hazard rules.)

Once a ball is declared unplayable, there are three options:

1. Play a ball as nearly as possible from where the ball was last played.

2. Drop a ball behind the spot where the ball lay, anywhere along an imaginary line demarcated by that point and the hole. There is no limit to how far back the ball may be dropped.

3. Drop a ball within two club-lengths of the spot where the ball lay (no nearer to the hole).

If your ball is in a bunker, a restriction applies to options (2) and (3). The ball must be dropped in the bunker. Recalling the pot-bunker scenario discussed earlier, the player would not have the option of dropping the ball behind the bunker. The only way to escape playing from the bunker is to play from where the ball was last played (like Mike's putt in the example above).

However, option (2) might make sense if your ball was plugged in the face of a bunker, and you see virtually no way of extricating the ball. It might make sense to take the penalty stroke and drop the ball at the rear of the bunker, rather than to rack

Always playable: Luke Donald comes out of a tough bunker lie.

up multiple strokes flailing away at the embedded ball. Again, knowing your options is essential to making rational decisions. And, if you're totally incapable of playing a bunker shot from even a decent lie, option (1) might make sense. You might hit the green, take one or two putts, and still be better off even with the penalty stroke. The unplayable ball rule lets you choose your battles.

Sometimes the options seemingly afforded by the unplayable ball rule prove to be illusory. For example, if your ball is in a wooded ravine, options (2) and (3) might not provide relief. Your only choice might be to return to the spot from which you last played. This equates to the stroke-and-distance penalty applicable to lost balls or balls hit out of bounds.

Obstructions

The Rules of Golf, unfortunately, don't provide relief from the most troublesome obstruction faced by casual golfers: our brains. The rules do, however, provide relief from certain "obstructions." This is an exception to the general principle that you must "play the course as you find it." Knowing the rules on obstructions can save you strokes.

Generally, obstructions are anything artificial, such as structures, artificially surfaced cart paths and roads, sprinkler heads, sprinkler-control boxes, distance markers, stakes, and some walls and fences. However, there are a few important exceptions. Any part of an obstruction that is out of bounds; any wall, fence, or marker defining out of bounds; or any construction that is deemed to be an "integral part of the course" is not an obstruction, and no relief is available. Perhaps the most famous "integral parts of a course" are the road and stone wall bordering the 17th hole at St. Andrews.

The rules differentiate between "movable obstructions" and "immovable obstructions." A "movable obstruction" is any obstruction that may be moved without unreasonable effort and without unduly delaying play or causing damage. The classic examples are distance markers, stakes marking hazards, ropes defining ground under repair, and rakes in bunkers. If your ball lies in or on the obstruction, you may lift the ball, remove the obstruction, and drop the ball (or place it if on the putting green) as near as possible to the spot directly under the location where the ball lay, but no nearer to the hole. If the ball does not lie in or on the obstruction, you may remove the obstruction. (Try to remember to replace any stakes or distance markers you remove.)

The nature of relief from immovable obstructions is somewhat different: since you can't move the obstruction, you are entitled to move your ball. Generally, relief is provided from an immovable obstruction if your ball lies in or on the obstruction, or if the obstruction interferes with your stance or the area of your intended swing. However, no relief is available from an immovable obstruction if your ball lies in a water hazard. (You can only blame yourself for being in that predicament.)

One of the most common misunderstandings about the obstruction rule is that, with one rarely occurring exception, no relief is available for interference with your line of play (or line of flight). The obstruction must interfere with your stance or swing. So, if that sprinkler control box blocks your shot to the hole, but doesn't interfere with your stance or swing, you're out of luck. (Local rules may provide line-of-play relief from certain "temporary immovable obstructions," such as grandstands, but not from common obstructions such as sprinkler-control boxes or pumping stations.) Playing a ball that is in close proximity to an obstruction might create a mental hazard, but the rules provide no relief for psychological obstructions. (See sidebar, A Physical or Mental Obstruction?, p. 132.)

The only case where line-of-play relief is allowed is when an obstruction on the putting green interferes with your line

Identifying Your Ball:
Do You Carry Binoculars in Your Bag?

The Kelly Incident

They say trees are 90 percent air, but experience teaches us that the solid 10 percent comes into play quite frequently.

While most golf balls that encounter trees deflect into the fairway, the rough, or an even more inhospitable area, occasionally a ball becomes lodged in a tree. Let's say you hit a shot into the heart of a bushy evergreen lining the fairway and don't see it emerge. A search of the surrounding fairway and rough yields nothing. You're sure it must be lodged somewhere in the tree. What are your options?

Unless you can find your ball in the tree, you must treat it as lost. This means that under the stroke-and-distance rule, you must go back to the spot where you played the shot, take a penalty stroke, and play another ball. The unplayable ball rule, which provides additional options, is not applicable.

What if you see a ball in the tree? Can you assume it is yours, and avoid the lost ball penalty? While this might seem to be a reasonable assumption, unfortunately, you must treat your ball as lost unless you can identify the ball in the tree as yours.

If you are able to identify your ball (e.g., by climbing the tree or using binoculars), you are entitled to invoke the unplayable ball rule. One option under that rule is to drop a ball within two club-lengths of the point on the ground that is directly below the ball. You will still incur a penalty stroke.

This situation arose at the 2011 Honda Classic, when Jerry Kelly's ball became lodged high in a palm tree. Kelly was not able to identify the ball using binoculars. However, a photographer took a picture of the ball with a zoom lens, and officials were able to detect Kelly's mark: a green line on the ball. He was permitted to drop a ball under the unplayable ball rule.

The Kelly incident demonstrates the importance of marking your ball to ensure identification. It also raises the question of how certain the identification must be. Conceivably, the ball could have belonged to another player who used a similar marking technique. However, as David Staebler, Director of Rules Education for the USGA, comments, "The game is one of integrity. The Rules presume players are honest and therefore rely on players to identify their own ball."

So, carry a pair of binoculars or a good camera. It beats climbing trees.

Jerry Kelly utilized a nearby photographer's Nikon to identify his ball, which was stuck in the branches of a tree.

of putt. Since sprinkler heads or structures are rarely placed on putting greens, you're not likely to encounter this situation. Keep in mind, however, that some courses might adopt local rules permitting line-of-play relief from sprinkler heads located on the aprons of greens, if your ball is within two club-lengths of the sprinkler head.

The first step in taking relief from an immovable obstruction when your ball lies "through the green" (anywhere other than the teeing ground or putting green of the hole you're playing, or a hazard) is to determine "the nearest point of relief." This is the nearest spot that provides relief from the obstruction and is not (a) closer to the hole, or (b) in a hazard or on a putting green. If your ball lies on the right side of a cart path, your nearest point of relief is to the right of the path, even if you'd have a better shot from the left. The second step is to drop the ball within one club-length of that point.

The rules state that when you are determining whether or not the obstruction interferes with your stance or swing, you must use the club you'd normally use for that shot. In other words, you can't pretend you're going to hit a driver for a 100-yard wedge shot and claim the longer club is in danger of striking the obstruction. However, if you are entitled to a drop for relief from an obstruction, you may use any club to measure your one-club-length relief.

If the ball is in a bunker, you must drop the ball in the bunker (or, under penalty of one stroke, behind the bunker). If the ball lies on the putting green, you may place the ball at the nearest point of relief, which may be off the green.

Knowing when you are entitled to relief from obstructions, and the proper method of relief, can save you strokes. Just remember that the rules in most cases don't provide complete relief, and there will be times when a structure or other obstruction blocks your line of play. In such situations, however, you probably didn't hit the fairway with your tee shot. As a rules official once remarked, "Bad luck has to start somewhere."

Provisional Balls

While many weekend golfers have an innate fear of water hazards, the penalty for losing your ball, or for hitting it out of bounds, is significantly more onerous. Under the "stroke-and-distance" penalty, you must take a penalty stroke and play again from the spot where you hit the errant shot. This can, in effect, equate to a two-stroke penalty.

The rule for balls that are lost or out of bounds is probably the most commonly violated rule among casual golfers. We've all been there. You hit your tee shot 250 yards into a problem area, but hope springs eternal. Surely, you'll find it. When you don't, are you really going to walk back to the tee and hit again, particularly on a busy Saturday morning with groups backed up behind you? Unlikely. You drop a ball, take a stroke, and move on. (You actually should be assessed a two-stroke penalty for failure to observe the stroke-and-distance rule.)

The remedy for this situation is to play a provisional ball if you think your ball might be lost or out of bounds. In the case of a tee shot, you'll be lying three if you ultimately have to play your provisional ball. Keep in mind that you must declare that you're playing a provisional ball. Otherwise, you'll be deemed to have put a new ball in play under penalty of stroke-and-distance and your original ball is deemed lost. If it appears your ball might be lost in a water hazard, you are not entitled to play a provisional ball. You must apply the water hazard rules.

Knowing the provisional ball rules can help you keep up pace of play and also provide you with some strategic options. You may continue to play your provisional ball up until the point on the course where your original ball was likely to have been lost or to have gone out of bounds. In addition, you still retain the option of playing your original ball if you find it in bounds. Even if you've played a provisional ball, you are not required to search for your original ball. You can abandon it at any time and play your provisional ball. However, if you find your original ball in bounds, you must play it. (See sidebar, Provisional Ball Rules and Strategies, p. 128.)

Abandoning your original ball might make sense if you play a great shot with your provisional ball. For example, if you hit your tee shot on a par-3 hole into the woods, and land your provisional ball two feet from the hole, it makes more sense to putt out for a 4 than to try to find and play your original ball from the woods. However, if you're in a match, your opponent is entitled to search for your ball! If it's found before you hole out with your provisional ball, you must play it.

One final point. It's essential to be able to identify your ball. If you play two identical Callaway 4s into the same area (your original and a provisional) and can't differentiate them, and ultimately find one of them, you'll be deemed to have found your provisional ball, not your original ball. Identifying your ball also permits you to invoke the unplayable ball rule, which often is more advantageous than the lost ball rule. (See sidebar, Identifying Your Ball, p. 122.) So do yourself a favor and mark your balls.

There is an apocryphal story about a debate between Joe DiMaggio and Ben Hogan about whether baseball or golf is the more difficult sport. DiMaggio observes that baseball players have to hit 90 mph fastballs, while golfers can tee up their ball. Hogan replies, "Yeah, but you don't have to play your foul balls." In an ideal world, we would find, and have to play, our foul golf balls. But we don't live in an ideal world. Play a provisional ball, and know the rules. The group behind you will be appreciative.

Luke Donald and his caddie, John McClaren, double-check their numbers before selecting a club.

Provisional Ball Rules and Strategies

What You Need to Know Before "Playing a Provisional"

Mike, Tom, Sue, and Ellen are playing a par-4 hole in stroke-play competition. Mike hits his tee shot into the woods. He says nothing, tees up another ball, and hits it in the fairway. Tom hits his tee shot roughly 275 yards toward out-of-bounds stakes, remarks, "I'm playing a provisional," and hits a second tee shot about 225 yards in the fairway. Sue hits into a ravine short of the fairway that is in bounds and not marked as a hazard, and Ellen hits her tee shot down the right tree line. They both declare that they're playing provisional balls and hit second tee shots in the fairway.

Mike finds his original ball, which bounced into the rough, and holes out in four strokes. Tom hits his provisional ball into a greenside bunker. He then finds his original ball in bounds, hits it onto the green, and two-putts. Sue does not look for her original ball, hits her provisional ball onto the green, and two-putts. Ellen finds her original ball in thick brush, decides it's unplayable, hits her provisional ball into a greenside bunker, and then blasts it onto the green, and two-putts. All four golfers tee off on the next hole. What is the result for each player?

Because Mike did not declare that he was playing a provisional ball, when he hit a second ball from the teeing ground he put another ball in play under penalty of stroke-and-distance, and his original ball was deemed lost. When he played the original ball from the fairway, Mike played a wrong ball and is penalized two strokes. Because he did not complete the hole with his ball in play, he is disqualified.

Tom scores a 4. Because he made the stroke with his provisional ball from a point farther from the hole than where his original ball was likely to be, his original ball was not deemed to be lost and the provisional ball did not become the ball in play. (Had Tom played another stroke with the provisional ball from the bunker before finding his original ball, the original ball would have been deemed lost.)

Sue scores a 6. She was not required to search for her original ball. Once she played the provisional ball from the fairway, her original ball was deemed to be lost and the provisional ball became her ball in play.

Once Ellen found her original ball, she was required to play it or invoke the unplayable ball rule. When she played her provisional ball from the fairway, she played a wrong ball and is penalized two strokes. Like Mike, she is disqualified because she did not complete the hole with her ball in play.

Vijay Singh gets the caddie provisional ball toss from his caddie David Clark at the 2011 BMW Championship.

Caddies and Rules

Avoiding Costly Penalties

Most of us these days ride in carts when we play. But what if you're playing with a caddie? Or are caddying? There are a number of rules that specifically address the role of the caddie and the player-caddie relationship. Knowledge of these rules is essential to enhancing that relationship and, more important, avoiding costly penalties.

A threshold question is: what is a caddie? The rules define "caddie" very generally as "one who assists the player," which may include carrying or handling the player's clubs. Of course, we all know that caddies do much more than carry clubs; they provide essential course information, help read greens, and provide input on club selection and strategy.

The rules also limit a player to one caddie at any given time. While a caddie may work for more than one player, a player may only have one caddie. However, not all types of assistance rise to the level of caddying. For example, if a player who employs a caddie also has a friend carry an umbrella or food and drinks, the one-caddie limitation is not violated.

Both the player and the caddie share the responsibility for knowing the rules. However, it is the player who pays the price — in penalty strokes — for any breach of the rules by his caddie. This means that the caddie must be extremely careful. For example, if the caddie lifts the player's ball in order to identify it without the player's authority, the player incurs a one-stroke penalty. Similarly, if the caddie neglects to remove an extra club in the player's bag before the start of competition, the player will be penalized for exceeding the 14-club limit.

This problem was never more evident than in the final round of the 2001 British Open at Royal Lytham & St. Annes. Welshman Ian Woosnam was just a stroke out of the lead when he teed off that Sunday afternoon, but when they reached the second tee (the first hole at Royal Lytham is a par 3) caddie Miles Byrne reached for Woosnam's driver, and felt all the blood rush from his head. There were not one, but two drivers in the bag. Woosnam had been experimenting with another type of driver on the range, and neither he nor his caddie had taken it out of the golf bag before beginning the round. The penalty for having more than 14 clubs? Two strokes. That was the end of Woosnam's attempt to win the tournament, and just about the end of the relationship between caddie and player (Woosnam didn't fire Byrnes right away . . he waited until the caddie missed a tee time a week or so later).

A caddie may perform certain acts without the player's authority. These include searching for the player's ball; repairing ball marks; removing loose impediments; marking the position of (but not lifting) a ball; cleaning the player's ball; and removing movable obstructions. A caddie should never lift the player's ball when it is in play.

When involved in a competition, a player may not give advice to anyone other than his partner, or ask for advice from anyone other than his partner,

Padraig Harrington and his caddie, Ronan Flood, know what the rules say a caddie can — and cannot — do.

his caddie, or his partner's caddie. This rule is violated if the player's caddie provides advice to a competitor. For example, if the player's caddie remarks to his opponent, "I think you're overswinging," the player is penalized.

A caddie may help the player determine his line of putt, but may not position himself on the line of putt, or an extension of the line of putt beyond the hole, while the player makes his stroke. In addition, the caddie may not touch the putting green while pointing out the line of putt.

Another common caddie mishap is accidentally stopping or deflecting the player's ball; this results in a one-stroke penalty to the player. A worst-case scenario: the ball strikes the caddie, who is standing in bounds, and deflects out of bounds. The player incurs both a one-stroke penalty for the deflection and another penalty stroke under the stroke-and-distance rule, since the ball is out of bounds. The penalty also applies to deflections off the player's equipment, so the caddie should take care to keep golf bags out of the line of play.

For instance, if the aforementioned Miles Byrne had laid Woosnam's golf bag down beside the first green, and Woosnam, say, had come out of a bunker on that hole too hard, his ball striking his own golf bag on the ground, he would have been charged with deflecting his ball and assessed a penalty. And poor Miles would likely have been canned on the spot!

INSIDE GOLF'S TOUGHEST SHOTS
A Physical or Mental Obstruction?

Charl Schwartzel and Sprinkler Heads

During the 2011 Memorial Tournament, Masters champion Charl Schwartzel was allowed to take relief from two sprinkler heads in the rough and drop his ball in the fairway. Some commentators felt that, while perhaps within the gray area of the obstruction rule, Schwartzel might have gotten a break.

On the par-5 13th hole, Schwartzel's tee shot came to rest in the first cut of rough left of the fairway, about eight inches behind and between two sprinkler heads. After a lengthy discussion, a PGA Tour rules official allowed Schwartzel to take relief, based on the player's contention that he might hit one of the sprinkler heads during his swing. Schwartzel was permitted to drop within one club-length of the determined nearest point of relief, which allowed him to play his second shot from the fairway.

The rules provide relief from an immovable obstruction if the obstruction "interferes with the player's stance or the area of his intended swing." There was no interference with Schwartzel's stance; the question was whether there was a reasonable possibility he *might* hit a sprinkler head after striking the ball. A player is not entitled to relief from a mental distraction caused by an obstruction; the obstruction must actually interfere with stance or swing.

"I was going to have to hit down on it to make good contact, so I was scared I was going to catch one of the sprinklers," Schwartzel said after the round, explaining the incident to the press. The PGA Tour official explained that "it was in that zone where interference is sketchy. He has to tell me; he's going to hit it. We did the practice swing and it was obvious he was going to hit it."

Some commentators thought the ruling was generous. One Tour player made the point that, with a 235-yard shot, Schwartzel was unlikely to take much of a divot (and, in fact, he didn't when he played the shot from the fairway). Another commentator observed that it appeared that only if Schwartzel had made an unorthodox, in-to-out swing would his clubhead have come anywhere near the sprinkler head.

Freed from his sprinkler-head angst, Schwartzel landed his ball 12 feet from the hole but missed the eagle putt, settling for a birdie. Justice?

2011 Masters champion Charl Schwartzel used the rules to get relief from a sprinkler head during the 2011 Memorial Tournament in Dublin, Ohio.

CHAPTER SIX
Caddie Wisdom, Inspiration, and Humor

Mastering Golf's Toughest Shots, like our previous book, *Think Like a Caddie, Play Like a Pro*, has attempted to present a look at course strategy, shot selection, and overall playing philosophy from a unique point of view: that of the caddie. Because of the ongoing trends in the game of golf, and despite a recent uptick in interest in walking a course with a caddie on the bag, most golfers in these early years of the 21st century have never had the experience of playing with a looper. Except for the holdouts of those venerable old clubs that still maintain a caddie corps, or a few fancy resorts that have outsourced their caddie program to a private company, most of us have spent our golfing lives riding in motorized carts.

That's too bad, on several levels. First, caddies have been an integral part of the game from its earliest days. Especially in heated competition, every golfer is entitled by the Rules of Golf to have a caddie, to carry the clubs and perform any or all of the following duties: swing coach, navigator, psychologist, joke teller, refreshment bearer, ball hunter, rules consultant, green reader, club and ball cleaner, and general factotum and boon companion. The good ones can deduce what club you should hit on a particular shot, read putts perfectly, and help steer you away from trouble. But even a mediocre caddie should be able to emit a few encouraging words after a bad shot, and a few of praise after a good one. And that sense of a shared enterprise between player and caddie — getting the ball around the course in as few strokes as possible — can be reassuring and liberating.

With a caddie, it's not "me" against the course, it's "us."

Of course, the decline in the use of caddies due to carts is regrettable for the game as a whole. An entire generation of golfers once got introduced to the game from the bottom up, working long summer days carrying two bags for fifty cents a loop. While one can understand the economics (a golf cart costs somewhere between $1 and $2 to operate per round; courses

135

Opposite page: Teamwork: Zach Johnson and caddie Damon Green have teamed up successfully on the PGA Tour since 2004.

get $20 and up in revenue), one can still lament the loss of this important tool for introducing new players to the game.

But what we've tried to show in these two books is that one of the most important roles of the caddie — course management and strategy — is something every golfer should consider before and during every round of golf. If you play with a caddie, you get the immediate benefits of a second pair of eyes, an experienced opinion on shot selection, and the important data that you need to successfully negotiate your way around a golf course. If you don't play with a caddie, you should try to gather as much of this on your own as you can. It's called *thinking like a caddie*, and that is oftentimes quite different from thinking like a player.

In this chapter, however, we're turning the microphone (or the word processor) over to the caddies themselves. With the help of the Professional Caddies Association (see Afterword, p. 151), we have interviewed dozens of professional caddies, both the old-timers ensconced in the PCA's World Caddie Hall of Fame, those working today on the professional tours, and those who work at private clubs. These caddies have seen a lot of golf over the years — good, not so good, and brilliant. Caddies, as is often said, never hit a shot nor put their name on the scorecard. Yet experienced caddies know a lot about golf, the golf swing, and the golf course — and, perhaps as important as anything, about the human condition.

In our extensive interviews with caddies, we came up with hours of tapes and pages of transcripts. And, along the way, we also collected some great stories about caddies, both famous and infamous, worth sharing. This chapter, then, contains some of the "outtakes" or advice we gleaned from caddies that didn't quite fit elsewhere in our book, but is still worthy of your consideration. And the stories . . . well, who doesn't enjoy a good caddie story? Even, or especially, those in which the caddies get some measure of revenge for having to follow us golfers up and down the fairways, in and out of the woods, and from rough to bunker.

GOLF PSYCHOLOGY

Hale Irwin was conservative by nature, but when it was the right time, he was totally aggressive. Hubert Green was more aggressive in general in his approach to scoring. So, you have steady guys who turn it on at times, and you have aggressive guys who back off at times. The player needs to know which type he is, and the caddie needs to know that, too.

— *Kenny Harms, now caddie for Kevin Na*

One thing you hear a lot is how important it is to block out the negatives. You leave a 12-footer three feet short for a three-jack and instead of fuming and cursing, you're supposed to put it out of your mind completely and walk real calm to the next tee. That's perfectly fine, but somebody has to remember that error for the next time the situation comes up. If the caddie thinks the player might half-hit the next 12-footer, he should say, "Okay, we didn't finish the stroke back on this same putt a few holes ago, so learn from that and make your adjustment."

— *Brett Waldman, caddie for Camilo Villegas*

The sports psychologists who write about pro golf make it sound like you need to have your emotions on an absolute even keel the entire day. That's not really possible, and it's not what happens in a golf tournament. Hitting accurate shots and making excellent putts are going to get the player and the caddie very pumped up. To me, that's natural, and it's okay to do. Look, we get excited out there. What you have to do is find a way for those emotions to go through you, and to use them for a positive energy. So yes, you can have emotional highs. Then you've got that couple of minutes between shots to even back out. You settle down, use the emotional energy in a professional way, and expect very good things from the next shot.

Actually, as a caddie, you have to keep those positive emotions flowing through you even if the round isn't going well. The way you know that you're doing that is when your player gets a very positive result from a so-so swing. The ball goes exactly where you wanted it to go, and you aren't surprised, you aren't shaking your head and talking about a lucky bounce, you're juiced up because, in your mind, the golf course owed you that. Your player has the talent, he makes lots of good swings that he doesn't get much out of, and now he's getting something back. So, immediately you and he are roused up and you're on the attack and you are just going to keep it up until the last putt falls in.

The one thing about getting pumped up is that eventually it will add distance to one of your shots, and both you and the player need to be ready for that. On tour, it generally doesn't happen until the last hour or so on Sunday, when you're in contention. But at some point you will be at 7-iron distance and you'll have to pull that 8-iron. So, you need to be smart about that.

— *Bobby Brown, former caddie for Dustin Johnson*

Rory [Sabbatini] is one of those rare players who can get angry and use it to his advantage. Sometimes anger helps put him right in "the zone," as they say. But he's not typical that way, so if a player can't get angry and channel it pretty naturally, the caddie is responsible for helping cool him down.

— *Kevin Fasbender, caddie for Rory Sabbatini*

There are lots of reasons why a player gets on golf course A and feels comfortable, and lots of reasons why he gets on course B and feels uncomfortable. When I'm with Boo [Weekley] on one of those course Bs, it's up to me to look for every possible reason why this course is good for us. You can start with the driving holes that you know will fit his eye and fit his natural shot. There are usually a few of those on any course. You can't completely just change a person's mind about a golf course, but you do what you can. And the amateur golfer can do that same thing to himself.

The other approach is to say, very simply, "Look, this isn't our type of course, and we won't ever go out of our way to come play here again, but let's win the tournament anyway. Let's shoot lights out even on a golf course we don't like — how cool would that be?"

—Joe Pyland, caddie for Boo Weekley

Playing an opponent who has your number: if an amateur is in a match against a player he hasn't been able to beat, the caddie and the player are going to be tested in terms of belief in themselves and belief in the player's ability. It's a situation that should bring you together and show how good a team you are, because that's when you have to push away all the doubts and really, really trust in the player's ability. The way to do that is to decide there is a good chance the other player just won't get his putts to drop. On each individual shot, you have to expect success; that's part of match play. But you keep an overall thought that "this isn't his day." And you put as much pressure on as you can. The key is belief in your ability.

— Craig Connelly, caddie for Paul Casey

THE CADDIE'S JOB:
GET THE YARDAGE

In the early 1960s, very few of us had regular caddies. At a tournament you took the caddie they assigned you, and there were some beauties. Bobby Brue slipped $10 to the caddiemaster once, hoping he'd get a caddie who knew what he was doing. On the first hole, Bobby asked the guy how far it was to the hole. The caddie answered, "About three blocks."

— Doug Sanders
Former PGA Tour player

Staying positive is crucial on the golf course. I am not saying that you should become an overnight optimist, but rather a positive-thinking realist. Sometimes you may not be hitting the ball as well as you would like. Rather than forcing the issue and attempting shots outside of your repertoire, play aggressively towards a realistic target. Identify three things you want to work on and improve, on your way to the golf course or driving range, and direct your attention on those items while you're there.

Stay positive and have fun. Golf is designed to have fun and experience great times with friends.

— *Mike Maher, WGA associate director of education*

During our Wednesday pro-am round at the 1998 Nissan Open at the Riviera Country Club, we played in a pouring rain. This was the first time Billy [Mayfair] had seen the course. I had walked the course on Tuesday, plotting our game plan.

Midway through the round, Billy literally said, "What are we doing here? I can't play this course." I told him if he would let me help him negotiate the course, we would be fine. Seventy-three tournament holes later, he was crowned champion.

— *Montana Thompson, former caddie for Billy Mayfair*

When the player is facing a difficult shot, you're always dealing with percentages. You have to gauge the situation, and the likelihood of the player pulling off the shot. This varies from player to player. The last thing you want to do is put doubt in the player's head, because then he can't commit to the shot. Some players are more aggressive than others. I try to keep the player in his comfort zone. But it's up to the player to make the decision and hit the shot. I've never seen a caddie's signature on a scorecard, or a caddie's name on a trophy.

> — *Jerry "Hobo" Osborne, longtime Tour caddie*

As we came off the 17th green, Seve [Ballesteros] said, "There's going to be a playoff." I said, "If we birdie the last, there won't be any need for a playoff." I think that got him thinking positive. That's exactly what he did, and he won the British Open.

> — *Nick DePaul, caddie for Seve Ballesteros*

THE FAME OF A CADDIE

Thomas L. Friedman, the Pulitzer Prize–winning *New York Times* op-ed columnist, foreign correspondent, and best-selling author, caddied, as a young man, at the 1970 U.S. Open at Hazeltine in his hometown of Minneapolis. His bag: the great Chi Chi Rodriguez.

Many years later, some friends of Friedman ran into Chi Chi at a Florida resort, and, knowing the story, asked the golfer if he remembered his caddie from that 1970 tournament.

Chi Chi thought a minute, then said, "Tommy!"

And did he know, they said, that his former caddie was now probably more famous than Chi Chi himself?

He thought about that, and said, "Not in Puerto Rico."

> — *Andy Martinez, longtime Tour caddie*

Do you remember Linn Strickler? He had Freddie Couples full time for a while. But he's working one week for Payne Stewart down at Harbour Town. And in the middle of Friday's round, Payne turns to him and says, "Hey Linn, how come all my yardages end in zero or five?" And Linn says, "I don't think you guys are that good. I just round them up or down.

If it's 162 yards, it becomes 160. If it's 163, it's 165."

— Mike "Fluff" Cowan, caddie for Jim Furyk

Sam Snead could be the king of surly to his caddies. I was out at the Senior tournament at the Newport Beach Country Club in California, and Snead asks his caddie, "Whadda we got?" The caddie tells him it's 147 yards to the pin. Sam hits it fat, and it goes into the front bunker. So Snead starts bitching out his caddie, "I hit that effin' ball 147 effin' yards and it went in the effin' bunker! What's the matter?"

And the caddie goes, "You hit it effin' fat!"

— Anonymous former caddie

A South African golfer hits his drive within one yard of where he hit his tee shot the previous day. He asks his caddie what he should hit, and the caddie says, "5-iron." Then the player asks, "What did we hit yesterday?" The caddie says, "6-iron." The player then proceeds to ask, "If I hit a 6-iron yesterday, why should I hit a 5-iron today?" The caddie replies, "Today, it's uphill."

— Anonymous former caddie

I once caddied for Mike Donald, and he was unbelievable. I noticed he was doing his own yardages, and of course I was doing my own. So we get to the ball and I say, "I've got 149 to the front edge." And he looks at his book and says, "I've got 151 to the front edge." So I say, "Okay, let's call it 150 to the front edge." And he goes, "No, let's call it 151 to the front edge."

— Andy Martinez, longtime Tour caddie

Michael Jordan, an avid golfer, has played many times at the exclusive Pine Valley Golf Club in New Jersey, where one of the star attractions is longtime caddie Rocky Carbone. Prior to the round Rocky handed MJ his business card, which read, "Rocky Carbone, Wind and Yardage Consultant."

On the first hole, Jordan had a 30-footer. He consulted with Rocky, who was his caddie, and then missed the putt to the right. Jordan pulled out the business card and waved it at the caddie, saying, "Hey, what's up?"

"Pro," responded Rocky, "take a look at my card. It don't say nothing about reading greens."

— *Anonymous Pine Valley member*

THE BEST CADDIE JOKE EVER

I was at a conference in Africa and it got done early, so I asked the person at the front counter about any golf courses. He motioned a cab for me and told the guy some directions. We drove deep into the jungle until we came to the course. I went into the clubhouse and paid my fees and rented some clubs. I met my caddie on the first tee and was a little stunned to see that he had my clubs on one shoulder and a rifle on the other.

The first hole was a par 4, pretty straight away and tree-lined, and I piped one down the middle. As I set up to hit my shot, a tiger came out of the trees and started charging at us. My caddie calmly set my clubs down, aimed, and dropped the tiger with one shot! I was definitely rattled but made par.

On the second hole, a dog-leg-left par 5, I was setting up for my third shot when a lion came out of the trees and came straight for us. Once again my caddie put the clubs down, aimed, and took the lion down. I hit my shot tight and made a birdie!

The third hole was a par 3, about 200 yards over water. I hit it to about 25 feet. As I prepared to hit my putt, a crocodile came out of the water and started running at us. My caddie stood still. I said, "Aren't you going to shoot him?" And his reply was, "You don't get a shot on this hole!"

THE EQUIPMENT

You treat the equipment with a lot of respect and care. For example, if you watch Tour caddies, they are constantly wiping the grips with a wet towel, then a dry towel. How often do amateur golfers do this? Pretty seldom. We do it many times a day. A Tour player shouldn't ever put his hands on a grip that isn't nicely cleaned up.

Once a month we go through the clubs, checking the lofts and lies, and making sure the shafts aren't dinged, if they're steel. We also check the putter loft every two weeks. The 10-handicap golfer won't be able to do this, but he should know someone who can measure his specs at least once a year.

— *Kenny Harms, caddie for Kevin Na*

STATISTICS

When people think about Tour players using stats, they usually mean the stats you see on the PGA Tour Web site — fairways hit, greens in regulation. We pay attention to that, but a lot of the time you keep your own stats, ones that are a little more specific. One place that the amateur golfer and his caddie might start is by keeping a stat on putts he leaves right of the hole and left of the hole. Not so much big breaking putts, but the makeable putts with a normal amount of break — a cup or so. The tendency is to keep missing on one side or the other. When you warm up the next day you'll want to focus on that. Get the tendency ironed out, so you aren't favoring either side.

— *Brett Waldman, caddie for Camilo Villegas*

CADDIE HUMOR

According to Jerry Stewart's book, *Pebble Beach: Golf and the Forgotten Men*, the Introduction of golf carts to the famed resort on Carmel Bay in 1953 did not go smoothly. The veteran corps of caddies at the resort instinctively knew that the new carts were a threat to their income. Luckily, they also discovered that if the hand brake wasn't set correctly, the carts could roll away. "Needless to say, they all ended up in the ocean," recalled caddie Roy Drocovich. Most of the carts disappeared into Stillwater Cove off the 18th hole; remarkably, none was pushed off the dramatic cliffs on the 8th hole. Drocovich soon found the flip side of the cart assassination program: "It was part of my job to retrieve the lost carts, so I'd have to strip down and dive in after 'em," he said.

PUTTING

Reading putts: The best caddie in the world is not going to be able to give a player good reads right away if he doesn't know the player's preferences. For instance, you've got to figure out whether your golfer wants a "cup speed" read — that is, one that's meant to die into the hole — or a read for a putt that is going to get to the hole with some pace left over. For starters, the caddie should know what the player's basic preference is. If his habit is to always roll his own putts at cup speed, he should know that. Then, they'll be in sync right off. If the player is always hitting firm putts, the caddie will have to read the line according to that.

— Brent Henley, caddie for Woody Austin

Whenever one of my players really needed a good read on an important putt, I always used the Nicklaus approach:

you survey the putt from the low side of hole, and then from behind the hole. Pay attention to the uphill/downhill grade and the grain of the grass.

— Jerry "Hobo" Osborne, longtime Tour caddie

Many amateurs play lag putts too aggressively. Rather than playing for a two-putt, they get too aggressive and often leave themselves an eight-to-ten-footer coming back. I like to look at the hole as if it's the size of a five-gallon bucket. The goal should be to get the ball within that radius, rather than trying to slam it home from 30 feet. That way you almost guarantee no more than a two-putt and give yourself a chance to roll one in every once in a while.

— Mike Maher, WGA associate director of education

We were playing the 4th hole, a par 3, in the first round [of the 1961 Masters]. I had a putt of about 15 feet left of the hole, going up to the hole. I thought I had to hit it to the left edge. Most of the time, I read all my putts. But this putt confused me. So I asked [Ernest] Nipper. He said, "Right edge," so emphatically. I wasn't so sure of that. All he said was, "Gary, if it doesn't break to the left, you don't have to pay me this week." Sure enough, the putt broke left into the hole. That made the difference in my confidence all week. I had somebody with me who could really help.

— Gary Player on his 1961 Masters win

WAR STORIES

Back around 1993, we were playing a tournament in Paris, and Phil [Mickelson] came on strong over the weekend. He broke the course record on Saturday and kept it going on Sunday, so we came to the 16th hole with a one-shot lead. He made a great putt for a birdie on 16, and then we were waiting for the other guys to finish. I told Phil I was going over to the next tee to check the wind.

Instead of trying to push through the crowd, I decided to cut down this embankment and walk under a tunnel to the tee. I tripped, went ass over teakettle, and rolled down the hill. Next thing I know, I'm looking up at these concerned French faces. I don't know what they were saying, but I think it was, "He's dead."

> — *Jim "Bones" Mackay, caddie for Phil Mickelson*

Once I was playing out in the Midwest somewhere, and I had this caddie — local fella who knew the course pretty well. Well, we're going along, and I ask him what club I should use on this shot. And he doesn't answer me. Turns and looks the other way. I ask him again. Same thing: looks away, doesn't answer. Well, I can't have this, so I ask him what's wrong. He told me that last week he had carried for Sam Snead, and Snead had told him to do one thing and one thing only: "When I ask you what kind of club to use, look the other way and don't answer!"

> — *As told by Gene Sarazen*

Uncle Gary and Me

What I Learned After Years on Gary Player's Bag

I started caddying for my uncle Gary when he was 53, an age when most of us think of retiring. During our time together, he won eight senior majors, and it was one of the best experiences of my life. Looking back, if I had to sum up why he was so great as a golfer, it would be attitude, confidence, belief in his game, and staying fit. His operating philosophy was pretty simple: always play the course, never let the course play you. I think that's essential for pros and amateurs alike.

As a caddie, you need to be both a tactician and a psychologist. You need to learn when to push your man and when to keep your mouth shut. I remember many occasions when we would step onto the tee of a very difficult hole, and my instinct was to play it safe. Uncle Gary would look at the hole with the pin tucked in the back of the green, and his instinct was to fire at the flag. I would be shaking in my boots, worrying that this shot could cost him the tournament, and he would calmly step up and hit it perfectly. In 2009, at the age of 73, he played in his final Masters. On the difficult 4th hole, a 245-yard par 3, Gary hit it just short of the green. Why? Because he knew he could make par from there. His attitude and confidence were amazing and still are.

We had a great relationship, and Uncle Gary taught me a lot about golf and life. As he got into his 60s, I remember him telling me that his goal was to shoot his age, which he did a lot. Here was a 60-plus-year-old man whose goal was to shoot in the low 60s every time he stepped onto the course. He didn't want to make the cut, or to shoot a respectable score: he wanted to *win*. That is what sets him apart from the rest of the field and makes him one of the all-time greats.

To be successful on the course, you need to understand how to manage your game and the course. You may hit 300-yard drives, but do you keep the ball in the fairway with a good angle to the pin? Gary Player is a master at putting himself in a position to make a birdie and avoid trouble. The top players all have great skills, but the true champions are the players who understand that the mental game is more important than the physical. If you play like Bobby Jones and Gary Player, you will be a winner.

— *Bobby Verwey*

Longtime great Gary Player had two regular caddies in his time: Alfred "Rabbit" Dyer and his nephew (left, above) Bobby Verwey.

Caddie Hall of Fame inductees: (left to right) Sam "Killer" Foy (caddie for Hale Irwin), Angelo Argea (caddie for Jack Nicklaus), Jim Clark (now a centenarian and longt at Baltusrol), and Alfred "Rabbit" Dyer (caddie for Gary Player), with PCA cofounder Laura Cone (standing).

A New Chapter for the Professional Caddies Association Foundation

The Professional Caddies Association was founded in 1997 by a former caddie, Dennis Cone, and his wife, Laura, to provide professional caddies and their families with educational training, better communication, income opportunities, medical benefits and a retirement plan. The organization was launched at the Tournament Players Club (TPC) after the death of Tour caddie Jeff "Squeaky" Medlin, who died of leukemia in 1997. Despite his long career caddying for the likes of Nick Price, John Daly, and others, Medlin had little in the way of savings or benefits when he died.

Cone, a former kid caddie and central Florida resident, was the past president of the Junior Golf Association of Central Florida and cofounder of the Evergreen Youth Foundation (dba) PCA Caddie Foundation. He received initial funding for the PCA from the Marriott Corporation, caddie Mike "Fluff" Cowan, and others. In addition to raising funds to benefit and assist retired caddies, the PCA expanded its mission to provide caddie training and certification through its educational programs held worldwide. Through its various programs, the PCA has helped educate and certify more than 12,300 caddies to date, helping to reinvigorate the game of golf's efforts to return to its roots as a walking game. Working with the PGA Credit Union, the PCA administrators have set up the PCA Caddie Benevolent and Retirement Fund to provide financial benefits to retired caddies.

Also in 1999, the PCA inducted the first class into the PCA Caddie Hall of Fame in St. Augustine, Florida, to recognize the important service caddies have provided to the game of golf for more than 500 years, and

(Left to right) Mike Maher, Mike Donovan (director, WGA). Mary Ann Sarazen, Dr. John Reynolds (Caddie Hall of Fame), and Dennis and Laura Cone, at the PGA Merchandise Show.

to both professional and recreational golfers over the years. Honorees include both active and retired caddies, longtime caddie masters at some of the world's foremost country clubs and resorts worldwide, and others who have supported caddies and caddie programs.

In September 2011 at a BMW Championship press conference, the PCA Caddie Hall of Fame was transferred to the Western Golf Association. Founded in 1899, the WGA is the second-oldest golf association in the United States (after the U.S. Golf Association, founded in 1895). The WGA conducts tournaments, including the BMW Championship, the Western Amateur, and the Western Junior, and sponsors the Evans Scholars Foundation.

The Caddie Hall of Fame, founded by Dennis and Laura Cone and the PCA Foundation, will also continue under the new leadership of the Western Golf Association, with Dennis Cone and Dr. John Reynolds of Club Car representing the PCA Foundation. New classes of deserving caddies and others will continue to be inducted every year, and a new facility is to be installed at the WGA's headquarters located in Golf, Illinois, near Chicago.

(Left to right) Mike Maher (WGA associate director of education), Laura Cone, Dennis Cone (PCA), Tom Dreesen (2009 Caddie Hall of Fame), and Jeff Harrison (VP, WGA) announce the transfer of the Caddie Hall of Fame to the Western Golf Association.

RECENT CLASSES OF THE PCA CADDIE HALL OF FAME:

2009 Hall of Fame Inductees:

Gene Sarazen Spirit Awards:

- **Oscar Bunn**, one of the members of the Shinnecock Native American tribe who built the golf course at Shinnecock Hills, was a caddie there and played in the 1896 U.S. Open staged at that course.

- **Tom Dreesen**, comedian, global caddie ambassador, former caddie at Ravisloe Country Club in Homewood, Illinois. He has never forgotten his roots and thanks the caddie days.

- **Harvey Penick**, started as a caddie at age eight, became Master PGA Professional, teacher to many touring professionals and author of *Harvey Penick's Little Red Book*, one of the best-selling golf books of all time.

- **Dr. William J. Powell**, the first African American to design, build, own and operate a golf course, the Clearview Golf Club in Ohio. A true gentleman and pioneer in golf.

- **John Shippen**, the first African American/Native American golfer to play in the U.S. Open, in 1896 at Shinnecock Hills Golf Club in New York. He played in four more U.S. Opens in 1899, 1900, 1902, and 1913.

Caddie Manager Division:

- **Mike Kiely**, for 40 years the caddie manager at Canterbury Golf Club near Cleveland, site of the 2009 Senior PGA Championship.

- **"Gorgeous" George Lucas**, who has been creating yardage books used by PGA Tour caddies for more than 32 years. A special guy!!

- **Jim Tanner**, caddie manager at the Pawtucket Country Club in Rhode Island for more than 50 years, and a mentor to hundreds of young caddies and golfers.

Bucky Walters Spirit Award:

- **Joe McCourt**, past-president of the Blind Golfers Association and the caddie and coach of Bob Andrews, 2009 Blind Golfers champion.

Lynda Barco Spirit Award:

- **Jim and Jackie Warters**. Jim was a golf writer, member of the Golf Writers Association of America, a mentor, and a supporter of the PCA Worldwide Foundation.

2010 Hall of Fame Inductees:

Gene Sarazen Spirit Awards:

- **Fred Corcoran**, One of the pioneers of golf, helping to found the Ladies Professional Golf Association, the World Cup of Golf, and the Golf Writers Association of America.

- **David Fay**, recently retired as executive director of the U.S. Golf Association after 21 years. Fay began in golf as a caddie at the Tuxedo Club in New York when he was 11 years old and has long been a friend of caddies and the game.

- **Chris Sullivan**, the founder of the Outback chain of steak houses. Sullivan grew up in golf, beginning as a caddie at age 12 and continuing while he was in college. He instituted a caddie program at his club, Old Memorial..

Caddie Manager Division:

- **Sonny Meike**, longtime caddie master and manager at Butterfield Country Club in Oak Brook, Illinois. Has given back to the game and helped many WGA scholars.

Bucky Walters Spirit Award:

- **Jack Smith**, a caddie/coach for challenged golfers with special needs, has worked with more than 180 patients from the James A. Haley Veterans' Hospital in Tampa, Florida, for more than three years.

Lynda Barco Spirit Award:

- **Laura A. Cone**, the cofounder of the Professional Caddies Association, has helped "keep the lights on" for caddies and friends throughout the world. Thank you, Laura! — Team PCA.

Dennis and Laura Cone, cofounders of the Professional Caddies Association, and now inductees to the Caddie Hall of Fame.

The 2011 Hall of Fame inductee in Chicago (to date)

Gene Sarazen Spirit Award:

- **Dennis M. Cone**, founder and CEO of the World Caddie Headquarters — PCA. As a kid, Dennis grew up at a golf course, shagging balls and looping because he had an abusive father at home. The members helped give him the love he shares today with the world.

ACKNOWLEDGMENTS

In a classic contribution from life's Department of Irony, a few months after the publication of the first editorial venture between the Professional Caddies Association and Sellers Publishing, *Think Like a Caddie, Play Like a Pro*, I found myself spending a summer working full time as . . . *wait for it* . . . a caddie. The business of writing foundered on the shoals of the Great Recession, and I couldn't find any other kind of job, so I presented myself at the venerable Newport Country Club, hard by the shoals of Brenton Reef, and began looping for cash.

Now, I had caddied before, professionally and otherwise, but to say that I gained new respect and admiration for caddies during that summer would be only partially true: I gained entrance into an entirely new world that my previous experiences as a caddie, mostly for some celebrity pros during journalistic enterprises, only lightly touched upon. Here I discovered the real world of caddiedom: the 4:30 a.m. cattle call; the stifling heat of the airless caddie shack; the strictly Darwinian pecking order; the Army-like "hurry up and wait" delays while the members ate their lunch; the good loops, when one knew that a C-note would be the reward for five hours in the hot sun; and the bad ones: the unnecessary round in a pouring rain, or the time a member's wife handed me a tip of exactly *two* dollars. (*"The caddie will at all times smile and be grateful."*)

So when it came time to create another book for Dennis Cone, founder of the PCA, and Mark Chimsky-Lustig, editor-in-chief at Sellers Publishing, I was primed and ready. Locked and loaded. And somewhat thankful, I think, that I could spend *this* summer indoors working at my primary craft.

Was it my summer on the course that made this book a bit easier to produce than the last one? I don't know. I'd prefer to think it was a well-oiled team that operated efficiently to help me get the job done. That team begins and ends with Dennis and Laura Cone at the PCA, powerful forces of nature who smoothed the way with Hall of Fame caddies, wrangled photographs from oft-reluctant sources, refused to let their optimism dim, and once again were rewarded with, I hope, an interesting book. My thanks also goes to Jack Ross, who wrote the chapter in this book on the Rules of Golf and provided plenty of other assistance and counsel along the way. Montana Thompson, a former caddie himself who now serves as the caddie coordinator for the PGA Tour, provided his insight and his contacts with the Tour's current loopers, both of which proved invaluable. My father-in-law, Bob Alshouse, put me up at his Texas home for a week so I could work on the book while I pretended to take care of him. Marilyn Allen, our agent at the firm of Allen O'Shea, helped us again to cross the t's and dot the i's, as well as providing some much-needed hand-holding along the way. And Mark Chimsky-Lustig and the entire team at Sellers did another magnificent job weaving our manuscript into publishing gold.

Finally, my heartfelt thanks, as always, goes to my wife, Susan, whose support ranged from helping me get unstuck from time to time, to leaving me alone when deadlines called, to cheerfully putting up with our increasingly penurious lifestyle. And she understands the caddie's code: it's only the next shot that really matters.

— *James Y. Bartlett*

I want to thank God; my mom, so special for her giving heart; and my wonderful RN wife, Laura. I appreciate all the love and guidance, inspiration, and support they've given me during my 21-year quest to honor the great stewards and kids of the game, the caddies. On behalf of the PCA Worldwide, Laura and I would like to extend our gratitude to everyone who has worked on this project: Jim Bartlett, the very talented writer and funnyman who has outperformed us all in bringing you another wonderful book; our new contributing author, Jack Ross; research looper Montana Thompson; and team PCA photographer Steve Dinberg, a "class act" who worked with our friend Payne Stewart for over 15 years.

A special THANK YOU to golf greats and PCA ambassadors Mr. Gary Player and his caddie/friend Alfred "Rabbit" Dyer, PCA Hall of Fame inductee, for generously contributing the foreword and preface to this book. We would also like to extend a big thank you to Dr. John Reynolds for his mentorship to the PCA, and to express our gratitude to all of the caddies and players who have shared their experiences that helped shape this book, as well our previous book, *Think Like a Caddie, Play Like a Pro*. As Mr. Player says, in life "we must listen to our inner caddie" — it is our very own Godly mentor on and off the course of life. Thank you to all the great caddies past, present, and future who have helped us understand the importance of this great game. After all, "if you have never played golf with a caddie, you have never played the game of golf."

Thanks to the many other friends and family who took time out of their busy schedules to help with this ongoing mission. My gratitude to the PCA Board of Trustees for overseeing the mission of the PCA and the

Professional Caddie Association founder and president Dennis Cone with his wife, Laura.

PCA Foundation since 1992, and to Grammy Award–winner, Michael Bolton, who recorded the song "Five Feet Away" by David Vincent Williams and Mike Geiger to benefit the PCA and charities worldwide. Thanks also to the media team, David Shumate, Jamie McWilliams for Hall of Fame support, the golf writers at GWAA, the UK team, Worldwide media, Joe Louis Barrow Jr., Steve Mona, and PGA Tour player Donnie Hammond, as well as the PGA of America, the PGA Tour, and the LPGA, who have all been wonderful supporters of the PCA over the years, as has the Francis Ouimet Scholarship Fund, the Western Golf Association, and many other caddie associations around the world that have helped with education and caddie training programs. Caddie on!

To my grandkids, who light up my life. To all the kids I have seen around the world carrying that big bag with a smile — you get my heart pumping to continue the mission to help the kids and the game. At the end of the day, "It's all about the kids." Please join the mission — visit www.PCAhq.com.

— *Dennis Cone*

James Y. Bartlett is the overall project editor and main writer for *Mastering Golf's Toughest Shots* and *Think Like a Caddie, Play Like a Pro*. A longtime golf writer and editor, Bartlett has also published four golf mystery novels (The Hacker series, Yeoman House Books) and five books of golf nonfiction. He is a former features editor at *Golfweek*, was editor of *Luxury Golf* magazine, and was executive editor of *Caribbean Travel & Life* magazine. He was the golf columnist for *Forbes FYI* magazine for 12 years, during which time he wrote about his caddie experiences with Jack Nicklaus and Arnold Palmer. He is a full-time freelance writer and editor now living in Rhode Island.

Dennis and Laura Cone are cowriters of *Mastering Golf's Toughest Shots* and *Think Like a Caddie, Play Like a Pro*. They are cowriters/publishers and cofounders of the Professional Caddies Association (PCA), The Caddie Association (TCA), and the PCA Caddie Foundation (PCA-F). Dennis is a seventh-generation Floridian, who left the business world in 1982 to serve until 1990 as president of the nonprofit Junior Golf Association of Central Florida (JGACF), an organization that has helped thousands of kids get into the game of golf and life, and also helped send four players to the PGA Tour, including Chris DiMarco. Laura was the former financial consultant at the World Trade Center, is an RN nurse, and past president of the PCA. Since 1997, the PCA has helped educate and certify more than 12,300 caddies around the world. The PCA caddie-training manual has been used at more than 50 top country clubs, including Pebble Beach, Pinehurst, and a course in Augusta, and by the PGA Tour, and the PGA of America. The PCA, along with the WGA, sponsors The Caddie Hall of Fame (www.PCAhq.com) to honor noted caddies, from the past and present, worldwide.

Jack Ross, who contributed the rules chapter (Chapter Five) and assisted with other parts of the book, is a freelance golf writer in Massachusetts. Jack writes a rules column, as well as features, commentary, and course reviews, for *New England Golf Monthly*, and was a contributing writer for *Arnold Palmer's Guide to the 2011 Majors*. He completed an intensive PGA/ USGA rules workshop and has officiated at state amateur competitions. Several years ago, Jack decided to devote himself to two of his lifelong passions, writing and golf, after a twenty-year legal career in Washington, D.C., where in his spare time he taught his three sons to play golf on the public links of the District of Columbia (without caddies). He holds degrees from Yale University (where he spent nearly as much time studying the Yale Golf Course as studying history) and the University of Virginia School of Law. Jack would like to acknowledge his appreciation to Dennis Cone and Paul Trow for their support and mentorship in his new career, and to Jim Bartlett for welcoming him on board as a contributing author. Most important, he would like to express his love and appreciation for his father, who had no interest in golf but took up the game (in a manner of speaking) just to spend time with him; and for his sons, Johns, Campbell, and Hale, who continue to inspire him with their achievements, character, and positive outlook both on and off the course.

Richard M. "Montana" Thompson, research editor for this book, has worked in golf for many years and is a scoring official for the PGA Tour Rules Committee. He has been a Professional Tour Caddie for Billy Mayfair, Scott Verplank, John Inman, and Rick Pearson, among others. A founding member and VP of the PCA, he is 1981 graduate of Western Illinois University (Bachelor of Arts - Communications). He and his wife, Le, also spend time working for CBS Sports' coverage of the PGA Tour. They reside in Santa Rosa Beach, Florida, with their son, Luke. Montana is a founding member of the PCA and a caddie's caddie. Dennis, Laura, and Team PCA appreciate his work and support all through the years.

Steven Dinberg contributed his amazing photography to this book. He offers his clients a creative vision, extensive technical skills, and an expertise that allows him to create exciting, cutting-edge images. Steve shot the legendary photographs of Payne Stewart's last victory at the 1999 U.S. Open, among many others, and from those images produced the "Tribute to a Champion" lithograph. Steve is the "official" photographer for the PCA in 2012.